Gift from
Robert France

03. 2007

PROFITABLY SOAKED

Thoreau's Engagement with Water

edited by Robert Lawrence France

foreword by Ann Haymond Zwinger

afterword by Roderick Frazier Nash

Peter & Martin

May all your "soakings"

in water or in wine)

prove profitable,

cheers

RF

GREEN FRIGATE BOOKS

Sheffield, Vermont

"As Robert France shows us in this exhilarating and thought-provoking book, Thoreau's visionary transcendentalism has its boots deep in the mud of experience; and it is this embodied vision that makes him so significant a seer for our dissociated times. Thoreau's deceptively gentle style belies a profound radicalism that invites us to cast off from our islands of imposed intellectual order and to immerse ourselves fully in nature's vitality and variety, inspiring us toward a fuller engagement with the natural world."

> *David Kidner, professor at Nottingham Trent University and author of* Nature and Psyche: Radical Environmentalism and the Politics of Subjectivity

"Thoreau knew that water can change the focus of the spirit. Thankfully, Robert France has perfectly captured and consolidated the Master's timeless work to bring Thoreau's essence alive. This handy volume can be opened and read at random while visiting Mother Earth's lifeblood, when we find the opportunity to connect with water, and be a part of its moments, whether it be a pond, river, or ocean. It is a collection of quotations that may offer surprise at the precise appropriateness of the casually chosen quotation. A reading from *Profitably Soaked* in the presence of water can spark a spiritual epiphany in ourselves, such as those that Thoreau himself sought and described with such commitment."

> *John Middendorf, professional river guide, international big wall climber, and equipment designer*

"Again I am impressed with how alive Thoreau was—and after one hundred and forty years—still is. How still and focused he could be. How much of his communion, recreation and travel involved being with ponds, lakes, rivers, and the ocean. How often wet he was! How in love with the world he was. And I thank Professor France's stimulating presentation, *Profitably Soaked*, for this gift."

      J. Parker Huber, author of The Wildest County: A Guide to Thoreau's Maine

"In terms of intervention, what knowledge, per chance would Thoreau have us bring to a cycle of culturally conditioned experience and the actions that arise from such conditioned states? And what knowledge would we descendents of Thoreau, the contemporary lovers of land and water, have to bring to the conscious construction of our sensibilities? My guess is that Thoreau would emphatically suggest knowledge born out of bodily experience with the natural world. In the present compilation of quotations, Thoreau charges us to walk, listen, look, and immerse ourselves. This is how we know. It is only with experience, with sincere immersion in the sensible world, that our bodies begin to know—and thus to inform our every step."

      Laura Sewall, professor at Prescott College and author of Sight and Sensibility. The Ecopsychology of Perception

"One would expect that an inveterate pondside dweller such as Henry Thoreau would have something to say about water. But who would have thought that he could be so ecstatic about the subject. And so eloquent. A fine assembly of Thoreau's thoughts."

      John Hanson Mitchell, editor of Sanctuary Magazine *and author of* Walking Towards Walden: A Pilgrimage in Search of Place

*Would it not be a luxury to stand up to one's chin in some retired swamp for a whole summer's day, scenting the sweet-fern and bilberry blows, and lulled by the minstrelsy of gnats and mosquitoes? . . . . Surely, one may as **profitably be soaked** in the juices of a marsh for one day, as pick his way dry-shod over sand. Cold and damp, —are they not as rich experience as warmth and dryness?*

Henry David Thoreau, June 16, 1840, Journal Vol I, 141–142

ROBERT LAWRENCE FRANCE, Ph. D. is a professor at the Harvard Design School where he teaches courses in water sensitive ecological planning and design as well as environmental theory. He is one of the world's leading environmental researchers, having studied organisms from bacteria to whales in locations from the High Arctic to the tropics. Dr. France has published over a hundred technical papers and has authored or edited four technical books in addition to serving as supervising editor for own series at Lewis Publishing/CRC Press on Integrated Studies in Water Management and Land Development. He is also the editor of *Reflecting Heaven: Thoreau on Water* (Houghton Mifflin, 2001) and the eBook *Water-Logged-In: A Dynamic Library of Aquatic Quotations from Thoreau's Descendents* (www.water-logged-in.com, 2001). A complete listing of his publications and current research interests can be found at www.gsd.harvard.edu/faculty/france. Originally from Manitoba near the beautiful and remote lakes of the boreal forest, Robert now lives in Cambridge, Massachusetts just a short twenty-minute drive from Walden Pond (the sort of statistic he well knows would make Henry aghast). He takes every available opportunity to follow Thoreau's wet peregrinations around Concord.

ANN HAYMOND ZWINGER is a highly respected naturalist and author of many books, including *A Conscious Stillness: Two Naturalists on Thoreau's Rivers* with Edwin Way Teal (Harper & Row, 1982); *Shaped by Wind & Water: Reflections of a Naturalist* (Milkweed, 2000); and the widely regarded classic *Run, River, Run: A Naturalist's Journey Down One of the Great Rivers of the American West* (University of Arizona Press, 1984).

RODERICK FRAZIER NASH is one of the most eminent cultural historians exploring human–nature relationships, and is author of *The Rights of Nature: A History of Environmental Ethics* (University of Wisconsin Press, 1990); and the seminal classic *Wilderness and the American Mind* (Yale University Press, 1973).

Both Ms. Zwinger and Mr. Nash spend much of their recreation time conceptually following in Thoreau's paddle-strokes as they engage western rivers.

For R. W Nero and distant boyhood memories
of blissful summer days spent on riverine
explorations into the boreal forest of Manitoba.

*Other roads do some violence to Nature, and bring the
traveler to stare at her, but the river steals into the scenery
it traverses without intrusion, silently creating and adorning
it, and is free to come and go as the zephyr.*

*Thoreau. A Week on the Concord and
Merrimack Rivers*

Library of Congress Control Number 2002101162
ISBN 0-9717468-0-x

First Edition
Printed In United States of America

> Green Frigate Books,
> P.O. Box 469, Sheffield, VT
> 05866
> www.greenfrigatebooks.com

Published by Green Frigate Books
Distributed by Chelsea Green Publishing

Thoreau, Henry David, 1817-1862
> Profitably Soaked: Thoreau's Engagement with
Water./ Edited by Robert Lawrence France; foreword by Ann
Haymond Zwinger; afterword by Roderick Frazier Nash;
book design by Kjersti Monson.

The cover illustration was created by morphing and reworking
two images: Mediterranee (Gotthard Schuh,1935;
Foundation Suisse pour la Photographie), and Henry David
Thoreau 1817-1862 (Benjamin D. Maxham, 1856; The
Thoreau Society).

Contents

*The power of Thoreau's engagement with water,
expressed as it is so vividly through the fluidity of his
prose, continues to draw in contemporary explorers to
an embrace of the liquid world as if caught in a
back-eddy of some time vortex. Few have been so
"haunted by waters"—to use Norman Maclean's
wonderful phrase—as profoundly as has naturalist
and "water-logged" nature writer, Ann Zwinger.
—RLF*

Foreword

I distinctly remember kneeling beside a canoe one chill morning, right hand clutching a thwart, left hand holding onto a paddle thrust into the muck for balance, and fervently hoping the canoe was not going to deflect out into the Assabet River, catch the current, and leave me with an unsolvable dilemma. I was in the midst of co-authoring a book with Edwin Way Teale, he writing about the Sudbury River, I about the Assabet, and we spent profligate hours canoeing both rivers, in my case even swamping in the Assabet and experiencing its swift current first-hand. Although almost twenty years have passed, my memories of the Assabet are as fresh as the mists rising off its surface on that cool morn-ing. In my concern then I wondered only briefly how many times had Thoreau found himself holding river and shore together, aware of the stream's pull, hoping to keep both feet dry and a modicum of dignity intact.

I was the stranger in a strange land, a westerner from dry country. Thoreau was the native and these rivers were a part of his daily world. He walked the shores of the Assabet, bathed in the Sudbury, canoed down the Concord. In that happily watered land he immersed, pud-dled, splashed, made ripples, bathed, watched frogs, cavorted, enjoyed, recorded. Thoreau never knew life without plentiful water. Thoreau's love of these gracefully joined molecules of hydrogen and oxygen runs through his writing on a continual basis, a gleaming watery thread. There's no small satisfaction in noting that the personalities of his three rivers remains much the same: the Assabet, a working river, used and useful; the Sudbury slower, more gracious; the Concord, greater than the sum of its parts, bigger and busier, a personage of a river going places and getting things done with too much current to paddle upstream against. Many of the mills no longer use water power or are closed, much of the pollution that came after Thoreau's time is in the process of being, or has been, cleaned up. Thoreau wouldn't feel too much a stranger today although I suspect he'd be insulted by the impingement of so many people—he'd be put in jail not for civil disobedience but for skinny-dipping.

He took full account of the way water formed his landscape, observed how it sculpted the valleys with meanders, scribed its binding banks. Probably no other writer has taken such note of water on a daily basis, reveled in its animation, submerged himself in its image. His observations of the rivers in different lights and weathers matched those of Monet, painting his water lilies. Thoreau's journal entries are virtual baseline data, allowing those of us who come after a glimpse into their history, a chance to see snapshots of them taken a century and a half ago. His lyrical descriptions as well as his precise notations make us more aware of the necessity of healthy streams and ponds in our own time.

Thoreau's journals, with their careful quotidian responses, are a huge part of Thoreau's splendid heritage, that close appreciation with words that ran through his fingers like water, that lay cupped in his mind like refreshment. He may have walked along the seashore but he never went to sea and he always returned to the fascinating freshwater of his own beloved rivers that, unlike the ocean that sloshes back and forth, ran in only one direction—downhill. The rivers' one-way journey, always going on and never coming back, is an unavoidable metaphor for life that Thoreau used again and again, finding in that shivering shining mirror sliding across the earth full subject for his musings. Most river people I know carry that Thoreauvian sense of union with flowing water, both psychological and physical.

In the *Journals* the constant reiteration of a series of quick observations, Thoreau's constant and continuous adventures with his rivers remind me of an artist's sketches: intimate, quick moments caught with an economy of line. The artist's mind-shoulder-elbow-hand-pencil connect with paper in a spontaneous and affectionate way; unlike the final finished painting based on such fragments, they are not overrefined, varnished thoughts composed for public consumption and to hang on a wall. Sketches, with all their tentative lines and erratic strokes, are the beginnings of understanding. Thoreau's masterful verbal sketches are the same quick charming studies that have the delicate balance of a Rembrandt sepia ink language. They are not meant to be polished finished products but the precious insight of a moment that will never come again.

These rivers were part of Thoreau's useful life, rivers he observed almost daily so that he saw subtle change and the difference anchored in the essence. His views weave together as a continuum for his life. Thoreau enjoyed that priceless ability to trace the same places over continuing and contiguous of time, the familiarity that breeds affection.

What Robert France has done in focusing on Thoreau's water musings is to interlace them into a new context all their own. Reflections that are as discrete as reflective drops of water become, in France's perceptive treatment, runnels and rivulets coalescing into streams of their own, and finally coalescing into that sheet of shining water that brought Thoreau such joy. All these decades later, we watch the same ripples, the same water lilies open, the same fish feeding, the same sinuous sedges, the same sturdy buttonbushes barricading the shoreline, reflections of the same red maples, the same puddling ducks, the same blooming arrowweed, and doing so, become aware all over again of the beauty of the rivers of our lives.

—*Ann Haymond Zwinger*

Like a metaphysical poet, he sought to jar us into a recognition of the uniqueness of the mundane that we have become inured to, spurring us to re-sense and re-experience the world around us.

Robert France, Reflecting Heaven: Thoreau on Water, 2001

Introduction

While studying bullfrogs, Henry David Thoreau would often stand silent and still in a wetland for hours on end, staring into the depths with such intensity that sometimes his puzzled neighbors thought him to be drunk. That he certainly was, but not in the way that they imagined. One neighbor, seeing Thoreau engaged in such activity in the morning, at noon, and again in the late afternoon, described him "standin' there just like as if he had been there all day, gazin' down into that pond." This odd behavior of Thoreau's was common knowledge in his native village of Concord. His friend Ralph Waldo Emerson once chided that if God had intended Thoreau to live in a swamp, He would have made him a frog.

In point of fact, Thoreau really did need water for both physical and emotional sustenance: "I should wither and dry up if it were not for lakes and rivers. I am conscious that my body derives its genesis from their waters." Many times he felt that there was an imperative of nature that somehow forced him to enter deep into relationship with water: "I am made to love the pond . . . as the wind is made to ripple the water," he wrote. When observing fish swimming, he actually felt himself becoming "amphibious," longing to join them in their watery world. And once, playfully engaging in the kind of word game he so loved, Thoreau went as far as to liken himself to being a god of water: a "Thor-eau."

For Thoreau, "the water on a lake, from however distant a point seen, is always the centre of the landscape." Rivers to him, like the ocean to Melville, were the literal medium of a spiritual adventure. Thoreau was continually occupied with a need for a close personal and passionate communion with water: "I must let the water soak into me," he stated. Once, when reflecting about Walden Pond while writing in his journal at a distant location, he wrote that he sometimes felt a deep "thirst for it." Water provided solace for Thoreau as well. Following his occasionally stressful associations with his fellow humans, he often wished "again to participate in the serenity of nature, to share the happiness of the river."

Thoreau was fortunate to live in Concord, a location ideal to fostering his hydrophilic development: "It is well to have some water in your neighbourhood," he wrote, "to give buoyancy to and float the earth." The region's geomorphology and resulting scenery, shaped by the carving actions of glaciers, are very much part of a watery world. Indeed, at one time shortly after the Wisconsin Ice Age, the entire area was occupied by a single large lake. Large blocks of residual ice slowly melted to form the many kettle lakes such as Walden Pond that presently adorn the landscape. Meltwater also cut channels to create the major rivers—the Assabet and the Sudbury which interlink to form the Concord, as well as the many small streams that cross the land. Even today, following centuries of agricultural activity, wetlands comprise about a fifth of the total land surface area. Above all, it is Concord's riparian landscapes—the riverine, wetland, and lake shorelines—that present its most scenic feature. This situation was particularly true in Thoreau's day, when much of the uplands had been cleared of their forests.

Thoreau's life was bounded by water. He always associated himself with it: "I was born upon thy bank, river/ My blood flows in thy stream/ And thou meanderest forever/ At the bottom of my dream." One of his earliest memories was of visiting Walden Pond: "When I was four years old as I well remember, I was brought from Boston to this my native town, through these very woods and this field, to the pond." In one of Thoreau's last journal entries made when his view of nature consisted of only that which could be glimpsed from his deathbed, he focused on the furrows made by rain on the windowpane: "all . . . perfectly distinct to an observant eye, and yet could easily pass unnoticed by most." And among the very last words he ever spoke were: "Now comes good sailing."

Thoreau's fascination with the aquatic world involved several different forms of investigation: nature idolized (transcendentalism), nature idealized (aesthetic appreciation), nature itemized (scientific study), and nature lionized (environmentalism). The method Thoreau most often employed in his study of water—whether aesthetic, transcendental or scientific, involved his direct and purposeful exposure to and immersion in the medium itself. Thoreau, for example, believed that if one wanted to understand a swamp, it was not enough to merely look at it and intellectualize about it; instead, for true wisdom, one had to enter into and become one with the swamp itself through physical contact.

In a way this overall progression of Thoreau's method of investigation can be likened to a spatial template or a phenomenological progression in terms of experiencing water. First, the distant contemplative appraisals, using water as symbol—an affair of the intellect. Then, a closer examination of the aesthetic beauty of light and water, fostering loving reverence for the working of a presumed grand hydrological union—an affair of the heart. And finally, a very close immersion in water and a reveling in the simple joy of physical contact with nature—an affair of the body.

It is precisely this inter-coupling of mind, body, and soul, and the easy movement among each, where Thoreau reigns supreme among nature writers. His approach to nature was multifaceted: mystical communion, aesthetic pleasure, scientific insight, and physical exhilaration. A lover of truth and beauty, he strove to fuse the views of naturalist, poet, and moralist with an absolute desire to live life to the fullest, using his body as the barometer through which to experience and engage the world, thereby increasing his own understanding of it and his own role in it.

After a century of mythologizing and misunderstanding the man, Thoreau scholarship is currently undergoing a major change. Gradually the image of Thoreau as the mystical hermit of Walden, with starry eyes and, Saint Francis-like, a bird on his finger or shoulder, is being altered. In recent years, for example, Thoreau has come to be recognized as a working natural scientist. The purpose of the present book is to acknowledge that Thoreau, often compared unfavorably to his well-known descendant—the spirited sensualist Edward Abbey—was ever as much alive, particularly so given the muted mores characteristic of his own time. "I stand in awe of my body," he intoned, continuing "What is the Titan that has possession of me? Talk of mysteries! —Think of our life in nature, —daily to be shown matter, to come in contact with it . . . the solid earth! the actual world! the common sense! Contact! Contact!"

It was water, more than any other element, that was the means through which Thoreau made contact with the world. He enjoyed its presence in his life as a profound force of true recreation—recreation for the heart and soul as much as for the body. In this respect, the subtitle of Robert Richardson's otherwise wonderful biography of Thoreau, *A Life of the Mind*, misses the mark as an accurate description of Thoreau's full existence.

Book Scope

This book is part of an intended trilogy about the many ways in which water influenced Thoreau's life and work. The first volume, *Reflecting Heaven: Thoreau on Water*, focused solely on the more distant and abstract aspects of Thoreau's relationship with water: the aesthetic reflections of light upon water ("heaven is under our feet as well as over our heads"), and the transcendental reflections of life while regarding water ("water indeed reflects heaven because my mind does"). The intended third volume, *Singular Element, Interestingly Strange*, will explore Thoreau's detailed observations of water from a scientific perspective.

The present volume then is restricted to describing Thoreau's deliberate exposure to water—in other words, his direct immersion in the aquatic world. This is the first compilation of Thoreau's writings that concern his physical engagement with water in lakes, rivers, wetlands, springs, ephemeral pools, and the ocean, as motivated by his pressing desire for contact and recreation.

Anyone involved in Thoreau scholarship quickly realizes that, above all else, his was a varied life filled to the brim with complex thought and prose. Robert Schneider's introduction to *Thoreau's Sense of Place*, a collection of essays, provides an apt view of the difficulties of fully understanding the essence of Thoreau's place in the landscape of our modern environmental consciousness: "No single volume, no matter how varied its contents, can capture the full complexity of Thoreau's interest in place or the wide range of his influence on later writers. But the hope is that this volume will point toward some fascinating new directions in our reading of Thoreau and of his many 'sons and daughters' in the tradition of American environmental writing." I echo that wish here.

Thoreau's *Journal,* covering the years from 1837 to 1862, represents a considerable challenge for scholars, not the least of which is due to its voluminous size: seven thousand pages of over two million words. For the general public, few have had or will have the patience needed to carefully wade through all twelve volumes. This is a shame, for judging Thoreau solely by his more accessible works, *Walden* in particular, but also *Cape Cod* and *A Week on the Concord and Merrimack Rivers,* may produce an incomplete and inaccurate conception about what motivated the man, and what his ultimate message to us was. For it is in his *Journal* where Thoreau is found at his very best as an observer and recorder of the minutiae of nature, both natural and human/cultural (and it must be added, also at his very worst—a solipsistic and difficult friend, a misanthropic and petty bigot, and so on).

There is a great utility then in presenting the heart of Thoreau's wisdom as culled from his complete writings, including that of the *Journal.* Oddly though, given the dramatic importance that water played in shaping Thoreau's life and his writings, such "thematic Thoreau" volumes have hitherto concentrated on other topics. We have "Thoreau and birds," "Thoreau and Native Amerindians," "Thoreau and plants," "Thoreau and education," "Thoreau and mountains," "Thoreau and science," "Thoreau and landscape," and so on. However, until the present volume, in addition to an earlier book edited by myself and dealing with transcendental and aesthetic reflections, never a "Thoreau and *all* water" (*all,* because there have been several previous volumes that have dealt in a much more limited way with either rivers or the seacoast alone). Perhaps it is the vast extent of the material that has dissuaded anyone from undertaking such a task. Again, this is disheartening, for it was water above all else that most enraptured Thoreau: "What a singular element is this water!" he exclaimed in his *Journal.* Through contact and recreation with water, Thoreau was able to satiate his lifelong hunger for wholeness, his desire above all else to feel truly alive by tasting, touching, hearing, feeling, and smelling the aquatic world about him.

The following quotations, originating from all of Thoreau's works, have been grouped into thematic chapters by category of experience. First, in "Adventure," Thoreau engages in a romantic, sometimes endearingly childlike, fiction wherein his watery exploits take on occasionally mythic proportions: "[rivers] are a constant lure, when they flow by our doors, to distant enterprise and adventure." In "Joy," we find Thoreau reveling in a life of close association with water: "How much would be subtracted from the day if the water was taken away!" In "Contact," we observe Thoreau in his most intimate relationship with water: "He cannot be said to live who does not get pure water." And lastly, in "Contemplation," Thoreau uses the three previous perspectives as a means for reflecting upon the world around him: "In these degenerate days of man; who hears the rippling of the rivers will not utterly despair of anything." Together this corpus goes far toward educating us about the wonders of water, a job that Thoreau certainly believed himself ably suited to engage in: "We are slow to realize water—the beauty and magic of it," he once instructed.

Moving From Words to Action: Personally Applying the Message

Reading a book, no matter how inspiring, is no substitute for direct experience. Thoreau certainly recognized this, and devoted equal time spent for reading and writing about, and time spent for actively exploring and deeply immersing himself within, nature. Reading the present book of quotations will work best whilst *engaged* in relationship with the very element they describe, rather than imagining it from the sequestered distance of a comfortable (and dry) arm chair. In an open letter to readers of *Orion Magazine*, several modern nature writers cautioned: "Words on a page do not accomplish anything by themselves; but words taken to heart, carried in mind, may lead to action." Therefore, throw this slim volume in a backpack and go out for a sail, paddle, or a swim, or if you are fortunate enough to live in one of those all-too-rare regions where it is still possible to drink the natural waters, do so. Then pull out this book, find an appropriate and inspiring quotation by Thoreau, and see if magic may happen, as it did once so memorably for me.

I still clearly remember that summer day almost a quarter of a century ago when, taking a break from my thesis work on limnology (aquatic science), I paddled out to the middle of "my" study lake and spent a glorious, life-transforming several hours drifting about and reading *Walden* for the first time. Coming to the particular section where Thoreau describes his own dreamy drifting about "his" pond in his boat, brought such a powerful feeling of temporal inter-linking that it has never been forgotten, and indeed has been the inspiration for so much else ever since.

It is only this direct and purposeful exposure to the ways of water, entering into what can be referred to as an "ecopsychological" relationship with the element, that will enable one's learning about both the external and internal frontiers. Achieving such a relationship is what Thoreau was really all about, describing his life's activities as being "nature looking into nature."

It is pleasant to hear the sound of the waves and feel the surging of the boat, —an inspiriting sound, as if you were bound on adventures.

We were about to float over unmeasured zones of earth, bound on unimaginable adventures.

Adventure

THOREAU WAS OBSESSED with bravery and masculinity, seeking the union between the contemplative aesthete and the heroic man of action. He was much enamored by the mix of spiritual heroism represented by such figures as Walter Raleigh and Francis Drake. During his stay at Walden Pond, Thoreau even likened himself to Robinson Crusoe. He greatly admired the "spirit of adventure" of the French voyageurs when they left the safety of the settled coasts to head into the unknown interior. His library contained maps, atlases, coast surveys, and natural almanacs, in addition to journals of explorers' voyages. He particularly loved accounts of the hardships suffered in the magnificent polar wilderness.

During his sojourns to Maine, Thoreau would sometimes envision nature as a hostile and dangerous River-entity with which he and his boatmen would grapple in order to move ahead. Camping once on the Merrimack River, Thoreau desired to read "the journal of some other sailor, whose bark had ploughed, perchance, more famous and classic seas." In his dreams, he imagined himself to be a Norse explorer sailing into the unknown. Occasionally, in his mind, these exploits took on a somewhat mythologized aspect of high adventure with him reveling in the thrill of danger. He loved engagement with the water world, welcoming the hardships and toil his adventures sometimes exacted upon his body as he struggled through swamps, lined up rapids, or paddled into choppy waves.

Although it is easy for us to smile in bemusement over the limited magnitude of Thoreau's actual explorations (compared to, for example, the intrepid derring do of those contemporary explorers of his whom he so admired), it is important to realize that what he was engaging in—namely the use of water as a recreation or leisure resource—was far in advance of the cultural mindset of his time. In those days, boating into the hinterland of Maine was a much more serious undertaking than it is for us today. To Thoreau's neighbors, even the very idea of going on a recreational trip to the remote backwaters of Maine was absurd, as only trappers and loggers (those who had to be there for their livelihoods) ventured forth into that dark, desolate, and dangerous wilderness.

Always fascinated by shipbuilding and all things maritime, when visiting Boston Thoreau would ignore the cultural delights of the city. Instead he was drawn to the wharves where he would engage in romantic dreams: "[I] sat on the end of Long Wharf . . . . As I watched the various craft unfurling their sails and getting to sea, I felt more than for years inclined to let the winds blow me also to other climes." Referring to the often flooded riparian meadows north of Concord as his own "green inland sea," Thoreau sailed his domain with unfailing zest and unbridled imagination: "I sail with a smacking breeze today and I fancy that I am a sailor on the ocean. It is an advantage that all towns do not possess." In his imagination, river towns became "havens," "ports" or "harbors." And even the smallest creek could be a fountain of adventure to foster wanderlust: "I am bound, I am bound, for a distant shore/ By a lonely isle, by a far Azore/ There it is, there it is, the treasure that I seek/ On the barren sands of a desolate creek."

For the first time it occurred to me this afternoon what a piece of wonder a river is - a huge volume of matter ceaselessly rolling through the fields and meadows of this substantial earth, making haste from the high places, by stable dwellings of men and Egyptian Pyramids, to its restless reservoir. One would think that, by a very natural impulse, the dwellers upon the headwaters of the Mississippi and Amazon would follow in the trail of their waters to see the end of the matter.

5 September, 1838, Journal Vol I, 75

What can be more impressive than to look up a noble river just at evening—one, perchance, which you have never explored—and behold its placid waters, reflecting the woods and sky, lapsing inaudibly toward the ocean; to behold as a lake, but know it as a river, tempting the beholder to explore it and his own destiny at once?

9 July, 1851, Journal Vol II, 320

It is pleasant to hear the sound of the waves and feel the surging of the boat, —an inspiriting sound, as if you were bound on adventures. It is delightful to be tossed about in such a harmless storm, and see the waves look so angry and black.

15 October, 1851, Journal Vol III, 73

Cut three white pine boughs opposite Fair Haven, and set them up in the bow of our boat for a sail. It was pleasant [to] hear the water begin to ripple under the prow, telling of our easy progress. We thus without a tack made the south side of Fair Haven, then threw our sails overboard, and the moment after mistook them for green bushes or weeds which had sprung from the bottom unusually far from shore. Then to hear the wind sigh in our sail, —that is to be a sailor and hear a land sound.

15 October, 1851, Journal Vol III, 74

We lay to in the lee of an island a little north of the bridge, where the surface is quite smooth, and the woods shelter us completely, while we hear the roar of the wind behind them, with an agreeable sense of protection, and see the white caps of the waves on either side. When there is a ripple merely in our calm port, we see the sunny reflections of the waves on the bottom, and the cranberries, etc. It is warm here in the sun, and the dog is drying his wet coat after so many voyages, and is drowsily nodding.

10 April, 1852, Journal Vol III, 397

All the fields and meadows are shorn. I would like to go into perfectly new and wild country where the meadows are rich in decaying vegetation and rustling vegetation, present a wilder luxuriance. I wish to lose myself amid reeds and sedges and wild grasses that have not been touched. If haying were omitted for a season or two, a voyage up this river in the fall, methinks, would make a much wilder impression. I sail and paddle to find a place where the bank has a more neglected look. I wish to bury myself amid reeds. I pine for the luxuriant vegetation of the river-banks.

31 August, 1852, Journal Vol IV, 329

Down river to Ball's Hill in boat.

Another perfect Indian-summer day. One of my oars makes a creaking sound like a block in a harbor, such a sound as would bring tears into an old sailor's eyes. It suggests to me adventure and seeking one's fortune.

25 October, 1852, Journal Vol IV, 399

The water washes against our bows with the same sound that one hears against a vessel's prow by night on the ocean. If you had waked up here, you would not know at first but you were there. The shore-lines are concealed; you look seemingly over an almost boundless waste of waters on either hand. The hills are dark, vast, lumpish. Some near, familiar hill appears as a distant bold mountain, for its base is indefinitely removed. It is very pleasant to make our way thus rapidly but mysteriously over the black waves, black as ink and dotted with round foamspots with a long moonlight sheen on one side—to make one's way upward thus over thee waste of waters, not knowing where you are exactly, only avoiding shores.

14 November, 1853, Journal Vol V, 504

What an entertainment this river affords! It is subject to so great overflows, owing to its broad intervals, that a day's rain produces a new landscape. Let it rain heavily one whole day, and the river will be increased from half a dozen rods in width to nearly a mile in some places, and, where I walked dry-shod yesterday a-maying, I sail with a smacking breeze to-day, and fancy that I am a sailor on the ocean.

29 April, 1854, Journal Vol VI, 228-229

I felt no little exhilaration, mingled with alight awe, as I drove before this strong wind over the great black-backed waves I judged to be at least twenty inches or two feet high, cutting through them, and heard their surging and felt them toss me. I was even obliged to head across them and not get into their troughs, for then I could hardly keep my legs. They were crested with a dirty white foam and were ten or twelve feet from crest to crest. They were so black, —as no sea I have seen, —large and powerful, and made such a roaring around me, that I could not but regard them as gambolling monsters of the deep. They were melainai—what is the Greek for waves? This is our black sea. You see a perfectly black mass about two feet high and perhaps four or five feet thick and of indefinite length, round-backed, or perhaps foaming a sharp ridge with a dirty-white crest, tumbling like a whale unceasingly before you. Only one of the epithets which the poets have applied to the color of the sea will apply to this water, —melainai, I was delighted to find that our usually peaceful river could toss me so. How much more exciting than to be planting potatoes with those men in the field! What a different world! The waves increased in height till [I] reached the bridge, the impulse of wind and waves increasing with the breadth of the sea. It is remarkable that it requires a very wide expanse to produce so great an undulation. The length of this meadow lake in the direction of the wind is about a mile, its breadth varying from a mile to a quarter of a mile, and the great commotion is toward the southerly end. Yet after passing the bridge I was surprised to find an almost smooth expanse as far as I could see, though the waves were about three inches high at fifty rods' distance. I lay awhile in that smooth water, and though I heard the waves lashing the other side of the causeway I could hardly realize what a sea I [had] just sailed through. It sounded like the breakers on the seashore heard from *terra firma*.

8 May, 1854, Journal Vol VI, 246-248

I improve the dry weather to examine the middle of Gowing's Swamp. There is in the middle an open pool, twenty or thirty feet in diameter, nearly full of sphagnum and green froth on the surface (frog-spittle), and what other plants I could not see on account of the danger in standing on the quaking ground; then a dense border, a rod or more wide, of a peculiar rush (?), with clusters of seed-vessels, three together, now going to seed, a yellow green, forming an abrupt edge next the water, this on a dense bed of quaking sphagnum, in which I sink eighteen inches in water, upheld by its matted roots, where I fear to break through.

22 August, 1854, Journal Vol VI, 467

It was quite an adventure getting over the bridge-ways or causeways, for on every shore there was either water or thin ice which would not bear. Sometimes I managed to get on to the timbers of a bridge, the end of a projecting "tie" (?), and off the same way, thus straddling over the bridges and the gulf of open water about them on to the edge of the thick ice, or else I swung myself on to the causeways by the willows, or crawled along a pole or rail, catching at a tree which stood in the water, —or got in.

31 January, 1855, Journal Vol VII, 158

At length, when the river turned more easterly, I was obliged to take down my sail and paddle slowly in the face of the rain, for the most part not seeing my course, with the umbrella slanted before me. But though my progress was slow and laborious, and at length I began to get a little wet, I enjoyed the adventure because it combined to some extent the advantages of being at home in my chamber and abroad in the storm at the same time.

22 April, 1856, Journal Vol VIII, 299

A withdrawn, wooded, and somewhat mountainous country. There was a little trout-pond just over the highest hill, very muddy, surrounded by a broad belt of yellow lily pads. Over this we pushed with great difficulty on a rickety raft of small logs, using poles thirty feet long, which stuck in the mud. The pond was about twenty-five feet deep in the middle, and our poles would stick up there and hold the raft. There was no apparent inlet, but a small outlet. The water was not clear nor particularly cold, and you would have said it was the very place for pouts, yet T. said that the only fish there caught were brook trout, at any time of day. You fish with a line only, sinking twenty feet from the raft. The water was full of insects, which looked very much like the little brown chips or bits of wood which make coarse sawdust, with legs, running over the submerged part of the raft, etc. I suppose this pond owed its trout to its elevation and being fed by springs. It seems they do not require swift or clear water, sandy bottom, etc. Are caught like pouts without any art. We had many bites and caught one.

6 August, 1856, Journal Vol IX, 502-503

The world is not aware what an extensive navigation is now possible on our overflowed fresh meadows. It is more interesting and fuller of life than the sea bays and permanent ponds.

22 April, 1857, Journal Vol IX, 333

Walden, I think, begins to crack and boom first on the south side, which is first in the shade, for I hear it cracking there, though it is still in the sun around me. It is not so sonorous and like the jumping of frogs as I have heard it, but more like the cracking of crockery. It suggests the very brittlest material, as if the globe you stood on were a hollow sphere of glass and might fall to pieces on the slightest touch. Most shivering, splintery, screeching cracks these are, as if the ice were no thicker than a tumbler, though it is probably nine or ten inches. Methinks my weight sinks it and helps to crack sometimes.

23 January, 1858, Journal Vol X, 251

When the ponds were firmly frozen, they afforded not only new and shorter routes to many points, but new views from their surfaces of the familiar landscape around them. When I crossed Flints' Pond, after it was covered with snow, though I had often paddled about and skated over it, it was so unexpectedly wide and so strange that I could think of nothing but Baffin's Bay. The Lincoln hills rose up around me at the extremity of a snowy plain, in which I did not remember to have stood before; and the fishermen, at an indeterminable distance over the ice, moving slowly about with their wolfish dogs, passed for sealers or Esquimaux, or in misty weather loomed like fabulous creatures, and I did not know whether they were giants or pygmies. I took this course when I went to lecture in Lincoln in the evening, reveling in no road and passing no house between my own hut and the lecture room. In Goose Pond, which lay in my way, a colony of muskrats dwelt, and raised their cabins high above the ice, though none could be seen abroad when I crossed it. Walden, being like the rest usually bare of snow, or with only shallow and interrupted drifts on it, was my yard, where I could walk freely when the snow was nearly two feet deep on a level elsewhere and the villagers were confined to their streets. There, far from the village street, and except at very long intervals, from the jingle of sleigh-bells, I slid and skated, as in a vast moose-yard well trodden, overhung by oak woods and solemn pines bent down with snow or bristling with icicles.

Walden, 175

Rivers must have been the guides which conducted the footsteps of the first travellers. They are the constant lure, when they flow by our doors, to distant enterprise and adventure, and, by a natural impulse, the dwellers on their banks will at length accompany their currents to the lowlands of the globe, or explore at their invitation the interior of continents. They are the natural highways of all nations not only levelling the ground, and removing obstacles from the path of the traveller, quenching his thirst, and bearing him on their bosoms, but conducting him through the most interesting scenery, the most populous portions of the globe, and where the animal and vegetable kingdoms attain their greatest perfection.

A Week, 9

I had often stood on the banks of the Concord, watching the lapse of the current, an emblem of all progress, following the same law with the system, with time, and all that is made; the weeds at the bottom gently bending down the stream, shaken by the watery wind, still planted where their seeds had sunk, but ere long to die and go down likewise; the shining pebbles, not yet anxious to better their condition, the chips and weeds, and occasional logs and stems of trees, that floated past, fulfilling their fate, were objects of singular interest to me, and at last I resolved to launch myself on its bosom, and float whither it would bear me.

A Week, 9-10

There were six of us, including the two boatmen. With our packs heaped up near the bows, and ourselves disposed as baggage to trim the boat, with instructions not to move in case we should strike a rock, more than so many barrels of pork, we pushed out into the first rapid, a slight specimen of the stream we had to navigate. With Uncle George in the stern, and Tom in the bows, each using a spruce pole about twelve feet long, pointed with iron, and poling on the same side, we shot up the rapids like a salmon, the water rushing and roaring around, so that only a practiced eye could distinguish a safe course, or tell what was deep water and what rocks, frequently grazing the latter on one or both sides, with a hundred as narrow escapes as ever the Argo had in passing through the Symplegades. I, who had some experience in boating, had never experienced any half so exhilarating before.

The Maine Woods, 31-32

It being about the full of the moon, and a warm and pleasant evening, we decided to row five miles by moonlight to the head of the North Twin Lake, lest the wind should rise on the morrow. After one mile of river, or what the boatmen call "thoroughfare," —for the river becomes at length only the connecting link between the lakes, —and some slight rapids which had been mostly made smooth water by the dam, we entered the North Twin Lake just after sundown, and steered across for the river "thoroughfare," four miles distant. This is a noble sheet of water, where one may get the impression which a new country and a "lake of the woods" are fitted to create. There was the smoke of no log-hut nor camp of any kind to greet us, still less was any lover of nature or musing traveller watching our batteau from the distant hills; not even the Indian hunter was there, for he rarely climbs them, but hugs the river fantastic sprays of free and happy evergreen trees, waving one above another in their ancient home.

The Maine Woods, 35-36

While it is river, you will not easily forget which way is up stream; but when you enter a lake, the river is completely lost, and you scan the distant shores in vain to find where it comes in. A stranger is, for the time at least, lost, and must set about a voyage of discovery first of all to find the river. To follow the windings of the shore when the lake is ten miles or even more in length, and of an irregularity which will not soon be mapped, is a wearisome voyage, and will spend his time and his provisions.

The Maine Woods, 37

While Uncle George steered for a small island near the head of the lake, now just visible like a speck on the water, we rowed by turns swiftly over its surface, singing such boat-songs as we could remember. The shores seemed at an indefinite distance in the moonlight. Occasionally we paused in our singing and rested on our oars, while we listened to hear if the wolves howled, for this is a common serenade, and my companions affirmed that it was the most dismal and unearthly of sounds.

The Maine Woods, 37-38

At last we glided past the "green isle" which had been our landmark, all joining in the chorus; as if by the watery links of rivers and of lakes we were about to float over unmeasured zones of earth, bound on unimaginable adventures.

The Maine Woods, 38

To avoid the difficulties of the portage, our men determined to "warp up" the Passamagamet Falls: so while the rest walked over the portage with the baggage, I remained in the batteau, to assist in warping up. We were soon in the midst of the rapids, which were more swift and tumultuous than any we had poled up, and had turned to the side of the stream for the purpose of warping, when the boatmen, who felt some pride in their skill, and were ambitious to do something more than usual, for my benefit, as I surmised, took one more view of the rapids, or rather the falls; and in answer to one's question, whether we couldn't get up there, the other answered that he guessed he'd try it: so we pushed again into the midst of the stream, and began to struggle with the current. I sat in the middle of the boat, to trim it, moving slightly to the right or left as it grazed a rock. With an uncertain and wavering motion we wound and bolted our way up, until the bow was actually raised two feet above the stern at the steepest pitch; and then, when everything depended upon his exertions, the bowman's pole snapped in two; but before he had time to take the spare one, which I reached him, he had saved himself with the fragment upon a rock; and so we got up by a hair's breadth;

The Maine Woods, 48-49

The bowman, not looking behind, but knowing exactly what the other is about, works as if he worked alone; now sounding in vain for a bottom in fifteen feet of water, while the boat falls back several rods, held straight only with the greatest skill and exertion; or, while the sternman obstinately holds his ground, like a turtle, the bowman springs from side to side with wonderful suppleness and dexterity, scanning the rapids and the rocks with a thousand eyes; and now, having got a bite at last, with a lusty shove which makes his pole bend and quiver, and the whole boat tremble, he gains a few feet upon the river. To add to the danger, the poles are liable at any time to be caught between the rocks, and wrenched out of their hands, leaving them at the mercy of the rapids—the rocks, as it were, lying in wait, like so many alligators, to catch them in their teeth, and jerk them from your hands, before you have stolen an effectual shove against their palates. The pole is set close to the boat, and the prow is made to overshoot, and just turn the corners of the rocks, in the very teeth of the rapids. Nothing but the length and lightness, and the slight draught of the batteau, enables them to make any headway. The bowman must quickly choose his course; there is not time to deliberate. Frequently the boat is shoved between rocks where both sides touch, and the waters on either hand are a perfect maelstrom.

Half a mile above this, two of us tried our hands at poling up a slight rapid; and we were just surmounting the last difficulty, when an unlucky rock confounded our calculations; and while the batteau was sweeping round irrecoverably amid the whirlpool, we were obliged to resign the poles to more skillful hands.

The Maine Woods, 49-50

The rest of the party walked over the remainder of the portage, while I remained with the boatmen to assist in warping up. One had to hold the boat while the others got in to prevent it from going over the falls. When we had pushed up the rapids as far as possible, keeping close to the shore, Tom seized the painter and leaped out upon a rock just visible in the water, but he lost his footing notwithstanding his spiked boots, and was instantly amid the rapids; but recovering himself by good luck, and reaching another rock, he passed the painter to me, who had followed him, and took his place again in the bows. Leaping from rock to rock in the shoal water close to the shore, and now and then getting a bite with the rope round an upright one, I held the boat while one reset his pole, and then all three forced it upward against any rapid. This was "warping up."

The Maine Woods, 52

Following up the course of the torrent which occupied this—and I mean to lay some emphasis on this word up—pulling myself up by the side of perpendicular falls of twenty or thirty feet, by the roots of firs and birches, and then perhaps, walking a level rod or two in the thin stream, for it took up the whole road, ascending by huge steps, as it were, a giant's stairway, down which a river flowed, I had soon cleared the trees, and paused on the successive shelves, to look back over the country. The torrent was from fifteen to thirty feet wide, without a tributary, and seemingly not diminishing in breadth as I advanced; but still it came rushing and roaring down, with a copious tide, over and amidst masses of bare rock, from the very clouds, as though a water-spout had just burst over the mountain.

The Maine Woods, 60

Though we glided so swiftly and often smoothly down, where it had cost us no slight effort to get up, our present voyage was attended with far more danger: for if we once fairly struck one of the thousand rocks by which we were surrounded, the boat would be swamped in an instant. When a boat is swamped under these circumstances, the boatmen commonly find no difficulty in keeping afloat at first, for the current keeps both them and their cargo up for a long way down the stream; and if they can swim, they have only to work their way gradually to the shore. The greatest danger is of being caught in an eddy behind some larger rock, where the water rushes up stream faster than elsewhere it does down, and being carried round and round under the surface till they are drowned. McCauslin pointed out some rocks which had been the scene of a fatal accident of this kind. Sometimes the body is not thrown out for several hours. He himself had performed such a circuit once, only his legs being visible to his companions; but he was fortunately thrown out in season to recover his breath.

The Maine Woods, 73-74

In shooting the rapids, the boatman has this problem to solve: to choose a circuitous and safe course amid a thousand sunken rocks, scattered over a quarter or half a mile, at the same time that he is moving steadily on at the rate of fifteen miles an hour. Stop he cannot; the only question is, where will he go? The bow-man chooses the course with all his eyes about him, striking broad off with his paddle, and drawing the boat by main force into her course. The stern-man faithfully follows the bow.

The Maine Woods, 74

The boatmen went through one of the log sluices in the batteau, where the fall was ten feet at the bottom, and took us in below. Here was the longest rapid in our voyage, and perhaps running this was as dangerous [and] arduous a task as any. Shooting down sometimes at the rate, as we judged, of fifteen miles an hour, if we struck a rock, we were split from end to end in an instant. Now like a bait bobbing for some river monster amid the eddies, now darting to this side of the stream, now to that, gliding swift and smooth near to our destruction, or striking broad off with the paddle and drawing the boat to right or left with all our might, in order to avoid a rock.

The Maine Woods, 76-77

We also paddled by turns in the bows, now sitting with our legs extended, now sitting upon our legs, and now rising upon our knees, but I found none of these positions endurable, and was reminded of the complaints of the old Jesuit missionaries, of the torture they endured from long confinement in constrained positions in canoes, in their long voyages from Quebec to the Huron country. But afterwards I sat on the cross-bars, or stood up, and experienced no inconvenience.

The Maine Woods, 96

It was inspiriting to hear the regular dip of the paddles, as if they were our fins or flippers, and to realize that we were at length fairly embarked. We who had felt strangely as stage-passengers and tavern-lodgers were suddenly naturalized there and presented with the freedom of the lakes and the woods.

The Maine Woods, 165

A very little wind on these broad lakes raises a sea which will swamp a canoe. Looking off from a lee shore, the surface may appear to be very little agitated, almost smooth, a mile distant, or if you see a few white crests they appear nearly level with the rest of the lake; but when you get out so far, you may find quite a sea running, and erelong, before you think of it, a wave will gently creep up the side of the canoe and fill your lap, like a monster deliberately covering you with its slime before it swallows you, or it will strike the canoe violently and break into it. The same thing may happen when the wind rises suddenly, though it were perfectly calm and smooth there a few minutes before; so that nothing can save you, unless you can swim ashore, for it is impossible to get into a canoe again when it is upset. Since you sit flat on the bottom, though the danger should not be imminent, a little water is a great inconvenience, not to mention the wetting of your provisions. We rarely crossed even a bay directly, from point to point, when there was wind, but made a slight curve corresponding somewhat to the shore, that we might the sooner reach it if the wind increased.

When the wind is aft, and not too strong, the Indian makes a spritsail of his blanket. He thus easily skims over the whole length of this lake in a day.

The Indian paddled on one side, and one of us on the other, to keep the canoe steady, and when he wanted to change hands he would say "t'other side." He asserted, in answer to our questions, that he had never upset a canoe himself, though he may have been upset by others.

Think of our little egg-shell of a canoe tossing across that great lake, a mere black speck to the eagle soaring above it!

The Maine Woods, 171-172

The following will suffice for a common experience in crossing lakes in a canoe. As the forenoon advanced the wind increased. The last bay which we crossed before reaching the desolate pier at the northeast carry, was two or three miles over, and the wind was southwesterly. After going a third of the way, the waves had increased so as occasionally to wash into the canoe, and we saw that it was worse and worse ahead. At first we might have turned about, but were not willing to. It would have been of no use to follow the curve of the shore, for not only the distance would have been much greater, but the waves ran still higher there on account of the greater sweep the wind had. At any rate it would have been dangerous now to alter our course, because the waves would have struck us at an advantage. It will not do to meet them at right angles, for then they will wash in both sides, but you must take them quartering. So the Indian stood up in the canoe, and exerted all his skill and strength for a mile or two, while I paddled right along in order to give him more steerage-way. For more than a mile he did not allow a single wave to strike the canoe as it would, but turned it quickly from this side to that, so that it would always be on or near the crest of a wave when it broke, where all its force was spent, and we merely settled down with it. At length I jumped out on to the end of the pier, against which the waves were dashing violently, in order to lighten the canoe, and catch it at the landing, which was not much sheltered; but just as I jumped we took in two or three gallons of water.

The Maine Woods, 186-187

The stream was only from one and one half to three rods wide, quite winding, with occasional small islands, meadows, and some very swift and shallow places. When we came to an island, the Indian never hesitated which side to take, as if the current told him which was the shortest and deepest. It was lucky for us that the water was so high. We had to walk but once on this stream, carrying a part of the load, at a swift and shallow reach, while he got up with the canoe, not being obliged to take out, though he said it was very strong water.

The Maine Woods, 210

The walking rapidly grew worse, and the path more indistinct, and at length, after passing through a patch of *calla palustris,* still abundantly in bloom, we found ourselves in a more open and regular swamp, made less passable than ordinary by the unusual wetness of the season. We sank a foot deep in water and mud at every step, and sometimes up to our knees, and the rail was almost obliterated, being no more than that a musquash leaves in similar places, when he parts the floating sedge. In fact, it probably was a musquash trail in some places. We concluded that if Mud Pond was as muddy as the approach to it was wet, I certainly deserved its name.

The Maine Woods, 215

We then entered another swamp, at a necessarily slow pace, where the walking was worse than ever, not only on account of the water, but the fallen timber, which often obliterated the indistinct trail entirely. The fallen trees were so numerous, that for long distances the route was through a succession of small yards, where we climbed over fences as high as our heads, down into water often up to our knees, and then over another fence into a second yard, and so on; and going back for his bag my companion once lost his way and came back without it. In many places the canoe would have run if it had not been for the fallen timber. Again it would be more open, but equally wet, too wet for trees to grow, and no place to sit down. It was a mossy swamp, which it required the long legs of a moose to traverse, and it is very likely that we scared some of them in our transit, though we saw none.

The Maine Woods, 219

Looking out I perceived that the violent shower falling on the lake had almost instantaneously flattened the waves,—the commander of that fortress had smoothed it for us so,—and clearing off, we resolved to start immediately, before the wind raised them again.

The Maine Woods, 237

Wherever there is a channel for water, there is a road for the canoe.

The Maine Woods, 246

This Webster Stream is well known to lumbermen as a difficult one. It is exceedingly rapid and rocky, and also shallow, and can hardly be considered navigable, unless that may mean that what is launched in it is sure to be carried swiftly down it, though it may be dashed to pieces by the way. It is somewhat like navigating a thunder-spout. With commonly an irresistible force urging you on, you have got to choose your own course each moment, between the rocks and shallows, and to get into it, moving forward always with the utmost possible moderation, and often holding on, if you can, that you may inspect the rapids before you.

The Maine Woods, 249

Before night we will take a journey on skates along the course of this meandering river, as full of novelty to one who sits by the cottage fire all the winter's day, as if it were over the polar ice, with Captain Parry or Franklin; following the winding of the stream, now flowing amid hills, now spreading out into fair meadows, and forming a myriad coves and bays where the pine and hemlock overarch.

A Winter Walk, 65-66

If I were a drawing-master, I would set my pupils to copying these leaves, that they might learn to draw firmly and gracefully.

Regarded as water, it is like a pond with half a dozen broad rounded promontories extending nearly to its middle, half from each side, while its watery bays extend far inland, like sharp friths, at each of whose heads several fine streams empty in, –almost a leafy archipelago.

But it oftener suggests land, and, as Dionysus and Pliny compared the form of the Morea to that of the leaf of the Oriental plane tree, so this leaf reminds me of some fair wild island in the ocean, whose extensive coast, alternate rounded bays with smooth strands, and sharp-pointed rocky capes, mark it as fitted for the habitation of man, and destined to become a centre of civilization at last. To the sailor's eye, it is a much indented shore. Is it not, in fact, a shore to the aerial ocean, on which the windy surf beats? At sight of this leaf we are all mariners, —if not vikings, buccaneers, and filibusters. Both our love of repose and our spirit of adventure are addressed. In our most casual glance, perchance, we think that if we succeed in doubling those sharp capes we shall find deep, smooth, and secure havens in the ample bays. How different from the white oak leaf, with its rounded headlands, on which no lighthouse need be placed! That is an England, with its long civil history, that may be read. This is some still unsettled New-found Island or Celebes. Shall we go and be rajahs there?

Autumnal Tints, 167-168

I do not know whether you think of ascending the St. Lawrence in a canoe—but if you should you might be delayed not only by the current, but by the waves, which frequently run too high for a canoe in such a mighty stream. It would be a grand excursion to go to Quebec by the Chaudiere—descend the St Lawrence to Fredickton, or further—almost all the way down stream—a very important consideration.

28 January, 1858, Correspondence, 506

The grand feature hereabouts is, of course, the Mississippi River. Too much can hardly be said of its grandeur, and of the beauty of this portion of it—(from Dunleith, and prob. from Rock Island to this place.) St. Paul is a dozen miles below the Falls of St. Anthony, or near the head of uninterrupted navigation on the main stream about 2000 miles from its mouth. There is not a "rip" below that, and the river is almost as wide in the upper as the lower part of its course. Steamers go up to the Sauk Rapids, above the Falls, near a hundred miles farther, and then you are fairly in the pine woods and lumbering country. Thus it flows from the pine to the palm . . . .

. . . After spending some three weeks in and about St. Paul, St. Anthony, and Minneapolis, we made an excursion in a steamer some 300 or more miles up the Minnesota (St. Peter's) River, to Redwood, or the Lower Sioux Agency, in order to see the plains and the Sioux, who were to receive their annual payment there. This is eminently the river of Minnesota, for she shares the Mississippi with Wisconsin, and it is of incalculable value to her. It flows through a very fertile country, destined to be famous for its wheat; but it is a remarkably winding stream, so that Redwood is only half as far from its mouth by land as by water. There was not a straight reach a mile in length as far as we went, —generally you could not see a quarter of a mile of water, and the boat was steadily turning this way or that. At the greater bends, as the Traverse des Sioux, some of the passengers were landed and walked across to be taken in on the other side. Two or three times you could have thrown a stone across the neck of the isthmus while it was from one to three miles around it. It was a very novel kind of navigation to me. The boat was perhaps the largest that had been up so high, and the water was rather low (it had been about 15 feet higher). In making a short turn, we repeatedly and designedly ran square into the steep and soft bank, taking in a cart-load of earth, this being more effectual than the rudder to fetch us about again; or the deeper water was so narrow and close to the shore, that we were obliged to run into and break down at least 50 trees which overhung the water, when we did not cut them off, repeatedly losing a part of our outworks, though the most exposed had been taken in. I could pluck almost any plant on the bank from the boat. We very frequently got aground and then drew ourselves along with a windlass and cable in an hour or 2, through the boat was about 160 feet long and drew some 3 feet of water, or, often, water and sand. It was one consolation to know that in such a case we were all the while damming the river and so raising it. We once ran fairly onto a concealed rock, with a shock that aroused all the passengers, and rested there, and the mate went below with a lamp expecting to find a hole, but he did not. Snags and sawyers were so common that I forgot to mention them. The sound of the boat rumbling over one was the ordinary music. However, as long as the boiler did not burst, we knew that no serious accident was likely to happen. Yet this was a singularly navigable river, more so than the Mississippi above the Falls, and it is owing to its very crookedness. Ditch it straight, and it would not only be very swift, but soon run out. It was from 10 to 15 rods wide near the mouth and from 8 to 10 or 12 at Redwood. Though the current was swift, I did not see a "rip" on it, and only 3 or 4 rocks. For 3 months in the year I am told that it can be navigated by small steamers about twice as far as we went, or to its source in Big Stone Lake, and a former Indian agent told me that at high water it was thought that such a steamer might pass into the Red River.

In short this river proved so very long and navigable, that I was reminded of the last letter or two in the *Voyages of the Baron la Hontan* (written near the end of the 17 century, I think) in which he states that after reaching the Mississippi (by the Illinois or Wisconsin), the limit of previous exploration westward,

46

he voyaged up it with his Indians, and at length turned up a great river coming in from the west which he called "La Riviere Longue" and he relates various improbable things about the country and its inhabitants, so that this letter has been regarded as pure fiction—or more properly speaking a lie. But I am somewhat inclined now to reconsider the matter . . . .

. . . The last of the little settlements on the river, was New Ulm, about 100 miles this side of Redwood. It consists wholly of Germans. We left them 100 barrels of salt, which will be worth something more when the water is lowest, than at present.

Redwood is a mere locality, scarcely an Indian village—where there is a store and some houses have been built for them. We were now fairly on the great plains, and looking south, and after walking that way 3 miles, could see no tree in that horizon. The buffalo was said to be feeding within 25 or 30 miles.

25 June, 1861, Correspondence, 619-621

Immortal water, alive even in the superficies, restlessly heaving now and tossing me and my boat, and sparkling with life!

The morning was a bright one and perfectly still and serene, the lake as smooth as glass, we making the only ripples as we paddled into it.

Joy

THE EMINENT THOREAU scholar and founder of the Thoreau Society, Walter Harding, concluded his biography: "Emerging from this long study of Thoreau, I find myself most impressed by Thoreau's aliveness." Thoreau took a boyish delight in running in the nude and ritually throwing himself into every water body he would encounter on his saunters. He celebrated the gift of life effusively: "surely joy is the condition of life," he exclaimed.

Thoreau was a land-locked mariner, thrilling to the feel of wind in the sail of his makeshift schooner as he plied the occasionally turbulent waters about Concord. He loved the physical exertion needed to negotiate not only the more or less tamed rivers of his neighborhood, but also the rough and rugged wilderness rivers of Maine. In contrast, his boating excursions on Walden and other nearby ponds were rituals to be slowly savored, sometimes entertaining guests by playing his flute, or when alone, leaning over the side to observe fish or other aquatic life. One of the most justifiably famous of all Thoreau's passages involves his description of engaging in a wonderful game of tag with a mischievous loon while rowing about Walden: "I found that it was as well for me to rest on my oars and wait his reappearing as to endeavor to calculate where he would rise; for again and again, when I was straining my eyes over the surface one way, I would suddenly be startled by his unearthly laugh behind me."

At no time, however, did Thoreau feel more alive then when he was exulting in the physical pleasure of the experience of skating on Concord's frozen riverine highways. Sophia Hawthorne, describing one such skating outing, contrasted Thoreau's "dithyrambic dances and Bacchic leaps on the ice" with her husband Nathaniel's sedately forward movement "like a self impelled Greek statue, stately and grave." Thoreau loved the speed of it, once clocking himself at the rate of fourteen miles per hour. And as for the polar explorers he so admired, winter for Thoreau, rather than restricting his peregrinations, provided him the means in which to extend his daily wanderings. On several days he would cover over twenty-five miles on his skates. Finally, when visited on his deathbed by a friend, Thoreau remarked: "You have been skating on this river; perhaps I am going to skate on some other."

And as we pushed it through the meadows to the river's bank, we stepped as lightly about it as if a portion of our own bulk and burden was stored in its hold. We were amazed to find ourselves outside still, with scarcely independent force enough to push or pull effectually.

1837-47, Journal Vol I, 439

The tortoises rapidly dropped into the water, as our boat ruffled the surface amid the willows. We glided along through the transparent water, breaking the reflections of the trees.

1837-47, Journal Vol I, 447

See ahead the waves running higher in the middle of the meadow, and here they get the full sweep of the wind and they break into whitecaps; but we, yet in the lee of the land, feel only the long smooth swells, as the day after a storm. It is pleasant, now that we are in the wind, to feel [*sic*] the chopping sound when the boat seems to fall upon the successive waves which it meets at right angles or in the eye of the wind.

10 April, 1852, Journal Vol III, 395

The river is my own highway, the only wild and unfenced part of the world hereabouts.

30 May, 1852, Journal Vol IV, 100

It is candle-light. The fishes leap. The meadows sparkle with the coppery light of fireflies. The evening star, multiplied by undulating water, is like bright sparks of fire continually ascending. The reflections of the trees are grandly indistinct. There is a low mist slightly enlarging the river, through which the arches of the stone bridge are just visible, as a vision. The mist is singularly bounded, collected here, while there is none there; close up to the bridge on one side and none on the other, depending apparently on currents of air. A dew in the air it is, which in time will wet you through. See stars reflected in the bottom of our boat, it being a quarter full of water. There is a low crescent of northern light and shooting stars from time to time. (We go only Channing's to the ash above the railroad.) I paddle with a bough, the Nile boatman's oar, which is rightly pliant, and you do not labor much. Some dogs bay. A sultry night.

15 June, 1852, Journal Vol IV, 105

After passing Hubbard's Bridge, looking up the smooth river between the rows of button-bushes, willows, and pads, we see the sun shining on Fair Haven Hill behind a sun-born cloud, while we are in shadow—a misty golden light, yellow, fern-like, with shadows of clouds flitting across its slope, —and horses in their pasture standing with outstretched necks to watch us; and now they dash up the steep in single file, as if to exhibit their limbs and mettle.

18 July, 1852, Journal Vol IV, 234

Paddled round the pond. The shore is composed of a belt of smooth rounded white stones like paving-stones, a rod or two in width, excepting one or two short sand-beaches, and is so steep that much of the way a single leap will carry you into water over your head. It is nowhere muddy, and the bottom is not to be touched, scarcely even seen again, except for the transparency of the water, till it rises on the other side. A casual observer would say that there was no weeds at all in it, and of noticeable plants a closer scrutiny detects only a few small heart-leaves and potamogetons, and perchance a water-target or two, which yet even a bather might not perceive. Both fishes and plants are clean and bright, like the element they live in. Viewed from a hilltop, it is blue in the depths and green in the shallows, but from a boat it is seen to be a uniform dark green.

27 August, 1852, Journal Vol IV, 320-321

To Walden.

Paddling over it, I see large schools of perch only an inch long, yet easily distinguished by their transverse bars. Great is the beauty of a wooded shore seen from the water, for the trees have ample room to expand on that side, and each puts forth its most vigorous bough to fringe and adorn the pond. It is rare that you see so natural an edge to the forest. Hence a pond like this, surrounded by hills wooded down to the edge of the water, is the best place to observe the tints of the autumnal foliage. Moreover, such as stand in or near to the water change earlier than elsewhere.

1 September, 1852, Journal Vol IV, 335

The forest has never so good a setting and foreground as seen from the middle of the lake, rising from the water's edge. The water's edge makes the best frame for the picture and natural boundary to the forest.

22 October, 1852, Journal Vol IV, 396

Returning, the water is smoother and more beautiful than ever. The ripples we make produce ribbed reflections or shadows on the dense but leafless bushes on shore, thirty or forty rods distant, very regular, and so far that they seem motionless and permanent. Again we see the mink, plainer than ever. The smooth river-reaches, so calm and glorious in this light, "I see, not feel, how beautiful they are." All the water behind us as we row (and even on the right and left at a distance) is perfectly unrippled, we move so fast; but before us, downstream, it is all in commotion from shore to shore. There are some fine shadows on those grand red oaken hills in the north. What a fine color to last through summer!

2 December, 1852, Journal Vol IV, 422

Loring's Pond beautifully frozen. So polished a surface, I mistook many parts of it for water. It was waved or watered with a slight dust nevertheless. Cracked into large squares like the faces of a reflector, it was so exquisitely polished that the sky and scudding dun-colored clouds, with mother-o'-pearl tints, were reflected in it as in the calmest water. I slid over it with a little misgiving, mistaking the ice before me for water. This is the first skating.

18 December, 1852, Journal Vol IV, 431

It is very pleasant to float along over the smooth meadow, where every weed and each stem of coarse grass that rises above the surface has another, answering to it and even more distinct, in the water beneath, making a rhyme to it, so that the most irregular form appears regular.

31 October, 1853, Journal Vol V, 464

As I paddle under the Leaning Hemlocks, the breeze rustles the boughs, and showers of their fresh winged seeds come wafted down to the water and are carried round and onward in the great eddy there.

1 November, 1853, Journal Vol V, 471

We rowed against a very powerful wind, sometimes scarcely making any headway. It was with difficulty often that we moved our paddles through the air for a new stroke. As C. said, it seemed to blow out of a hole. We had to turn our oars edgewise to it. But we worked our way slowly upward, nevertheless, for we came to feel and hear it blow and see the waves run. There was quite a sea running on the lee shore, —broad black waves with white crests, which made our boat toss very pleasantly. They wet the piers of the railroad bridge for eighteen inches up. I should guess that the whole height from the valley between to the top of a wave was nearer fifteen inches.

9 November, 1853, Journal Vol V, 490-491

The river was perfectly smooth except the upwelling of its tide, and as we paddled home westward, the dusky yellowing sky was all reflected on it, together with the dun-colored clouds and the trees, and there was more light in the water than in the sky. The reflections of the trees and bushes on the banks were wonderfully dark and distinct, for though frequently we could not see the real bush in the twilight against the dark bank, in the water it appeared against the sky. We were thus often enabled to steer clear of the overhanging bushes.

30 November, 1853, Journal Vol V, 532

It is remarkable how much power I can exert through the undulations which I produce by rocking my boat in the middle of the river. Some time after I have ceased I am surprised to hear the sound of the undulations which have just reached the shores acting on the thin ice there and making a complete wreck of it for a long distance up and down the stream, cracking off pieces four feet wide and more. I have stirred up the river to do this work, a power which I cannot put to rest. The secret of this power appears to lie in the extreme mobility, or, as I may say, irritability, of this element. It is the principle of the roller, or of an immense weight moved by a child on balls, and the momentum is tremendous.

3 December, 1853, Journal Vol VI, 6-7

Put on skates at mouth of Swamp Bridge Brook. The ice appears to be nearly two inches thick. There are many rough places where the crystals are very coarse, and the old ice on the river (for I spoke of a new ice since the freshest) is uneven and covered, more or less, with the scales of a thin ice whose water is dried up. In some places, where the wind has been strong, the foam is frozen into great concentric ridges, over which with an impetus I dash. It is hobbling and tearing work.

12 February, 1854, Journal Vol VI, 115

One accustomed to glide over a boundless and variegated ice floor like this cannot be much attracted by tessellated floors and mosaic work. I skate over a thin ice all tessellated, so to speak, or in which you see the forms of the crystals as they shot. This is separated by two or three feet of water from the old ice resting on the meadow. The water, consequently, is not dark, as when seen against a muddy bottom, but a clear yellow, against which the white air-bubbles in and under the ice are very conspicuous.

12 February, 1854, Journal Vol VI, 116

The sun being low, I see as I skate, reflected from the surface of the ice, flakes of rainbow somewhat like cobwebs, where the great slopes of the crystallization fall at the right angle, six inches or a foot across, but at so small an angle with the horizon that they had seemed absolutely flat and level before. Think of this kind of mosaic and tessellation for your floor! A floor made up of surface not absolutely level, —though level to the touch of the feet and to the noonday eye, —composed of crystals variously set, but just enough inclined to reflect the colors of the rainbow when the sun gets low.

12 February, 1854, Journal Vol VI, 119-120

We skated home in the dusk, with an odor of smoke in our clothes. It was pleasant to dash over the ice, feeling the inequalities which we could not see.

20 February, 1854, Journal Vol VI, 133-134

How dead would the globe seem, especially at this season, if it were not for these water surfaces! We are slow to realize water—the beauty and magic of it. It is interestingly strange to us forever. Immortal water, alive even in the superficies, restlessly heaving now and tossing me and my boat, and sparkling with life! I look around with a thrill on this bright fluctuating surface on which no man can walk, whereon is no trace of footstep, unstained as glass.

8 May, 1854, Journal Vol VI, 187

Skated a half-mile up Assabet and then to foot of Fair Haven Hill. This is the first tolerable skating. Last night was so cold that the river closed up almost everywhere, and made good skating where there had been no ice to catch the snow of the night before. First there is the snow ice on the sides, somewhat rough and brown or yellowish spotted where the water overflowed the ice on each side yesterday, and next, over the middle, the new dark smooth ice, and, where the river is wider than usual, a thick fine gray ice, marbled, where there was probably a thin ice yesterday. Probably the top froze as the snow fell. I am surprised to find how rapidly and easily I get along, how soon I am at this brook or that bend in the river, which it takes me so long to reach on the bank or by water. I can go more than double the usual distance before dark. It takes a little while to learn to trust the new black ice. I look for cracks to see how thick it is.

19 December, 1854, Journal Vol VII, 84-85

I am surprised to find how the fast the dog can run in a straight line on the ice. I am not sure that I can beat him on skates, but I can turn much shorter. It is very fine skating for the most part. All of the river that was not frozen before, and therefore not covered with snow on the 18th, is now frozen quite smoothly; but in some places for a quarter of a mile it is uneven like frozen suds, in rounded pancakes, as when bread spews out in baking. At sundown or before, it begins to belch. It is so cold that only in one place did I see a drop of water flowing out on the ice.

20 December, 1854, Journal Vol VII, 88

Skated to Baker Farm with a rapidity which astonished myself, before the wind, feeling the rise and fall, —the water having settled in the suddenly cold night, —which I had not time to see.

14 January, 1855, Journal Vol VII, 115

It had just been snowing, and this lay in shallow drifts or waves on the Great Meadows, alternate snow and ice. Skated into a crack, and slid on my side twenty-five feet.

15 January, 1855, Journal Vol VII, 116

The swelling river was belching on a high key, from ten to eleven. Quite a musical cracking, running like chain lightning of sound athwart my course, as if the river, squeezed, thus gave its morning's milk with music. A certain congealed milkiness in the sound, like the soft action of piano keys, —a little like the cry of a pigeon wood-pecker, —a-week a-week, etc. A congealed gurgling, frog-like. As I passed, the ice forced up by the water on one side suddenly settled on another with a crash, and quite a lake was formed above the ice behind me, and my successor two hours after, to his wonder and alarm, saw my tracks disappear in one side of it and come out on the other. My seat from time to time is the springy horizontal bough of some fallen tree which is frozen into the ice, some old maple that had blown over and retained some life for a year after in the water, covered with the great shaggy perforate parmelia. Lying flat, I quench my thirst where it is melted about it, blowing aside the snow-fleas.

1 February, 1855, Journal Vol VII, 161-162

The water falling, the ice on the meadow occasionally settles with a crack under our weight. It is pleasant to feel these swells and valleys occasioned by the subsidence of the water, in some cases pretty abrupt. Also to hear the hollow, rumbling sound in such rolling places on the meadow where there is an empty chamber beneath, the water being entirely run out. Our skates make but little sound in this coating of snow about an inch thick, as if we had on woollen skates, and we can easily see our tracks in the night. We seem thus to go faster than before by day, not only because we do not see (but feel and imagine) our rapidity, but because of the impression which the mysterious muffled sound of our feet makes. In the meanwhile we hear the distant note of a hooting owl, and the distant rumbling of approaching or retreating cars sounds like a constant waterfall. Now and then we skated into some chippy, crackling white ice, where a superficial puddle had run dry before freezing hard, and got a tumble.

2 February, 1855, Journal Vol VII, 164

Skated up the river with T[appa]n in spite of the snow and wind. It had cleared up, but the snow was on a level strong three quarters of an inch deep (seemingly an inch), but for the most part blown into drifts three to ten feet wide and much deeper (with bare intervals) under a strong northwesterly wind. It was a novel experience, this skating through snow, sometimes a mile without a bare spot, this blustering day. In many places a crack ran across our course where the water had oozed out, and the driving snow catching in it had formed a thick batter with a stiffish crust in which we were tripped up and measured our lengths on the ice. The few thin places were concealed, and we avoided them by our knowledge of the localities, though we sometimes saw the air-bubbles of the mid-channel through the thin ice; for, the water going down, the current is increasing and eating its way through the ice. Sometimes a thicker drift, too, threw us, or a sudden unevenness in the concealed ice; but on the whole the snow was but a slight obstruction. We skated with much more facility than I had anticipated, and I would not have missed the experience for a good deal. The water, falling rapidly, has left a part of the ice in shelves attached to the shore and to the alders and other trees and bushes, fifteen or eighteen inches above the general level, with a spongy or brittle mass of crystals suspended from its under sides five or six inches deep, or double that of the ice, looking like lace-work on the side and showing all kinds of angular geometrical figures when you look down on it turned bottom up; as if the water had sunk away faster than it could freeze solidly. I think that in my ice-flakes of the 2d the thin crust of the horizontal ice was blown off and had left these exposed. Sometimes we had to face a head wind and driving or blowing snow which concealed the prospect a few rods ahead, and we made a tedious progress.

We went up the Pantry Meadow above the old William Wheeler house, and came down this meadow again with the wind and snow dust, spreading our coat-tails, like birds, though somewhat at the risk of our necks if we had struck a foul place. I found that I could sail on a tack pretty well, trimming with my skirts. Sometimes we had to jump suddenly over some obstacle which the snow had concealed before, to save our necks.

3 February, 1855, Journal Vol VII, 165-166

The drifts will probably harden by to-morrow and make such skating impossible. I was curious to see how my tracks looked, —what figure I cut, —and skated back a little to look at it.

3 February, 1855, Journal Vol VII, 167

It is now good walking on the river, for, though there has been no thaw since the snow came, a great part of it has been converted into snow ice by sinking the old ice beneath the water, and the crust of the rest is stronger than in the fields, because the snow is so shallow and has been so moist. The river is thus an advantage as a highway, not only in summer and when the ice is bare in the winter, but even when the snow lies very deep in the fields. It is invaluable to the walker, being now not only the most interesting, but, excepting the narrow and unpleasant track in the highways, the only practicable route. The snow never lies so deep over it as elsewhere, and, if deep, it sinks the ice and is soon converted into snow ice to a great extent, beside being blown out of the river valley. Neither is it drifted here. Here, where you cannot walk at all in the summer, is better walking than elsewhere in the winter. But what a different aspect the river's brim now from what it wears in summer! I do not this moment hear an insect hum, nor see a bird, nor a flower. That museum of animal and vegetable life, a meadow, is now reduced to a uniform level of white snow, with only half a dozen kinds of shrubs and weeds rising here and there above it.

20 January, 1856, Journal Vol VIII, 121-122

I walk with a peculiar sense of freedom over the snow-covered ice, not fearing that I shall break through.

24 January, 1856, Journal Vol VIII, 136

Where a few months since was a fertilizing river reflecting the sunset, and luxuriant meadows resounding with the hum of insects, is now a uniform crusted snow, with dry powdery snow drifting over it and confounding river and meadow. I make haste away, covering my ears, before I freeze there.

25 January, 1856, Journal Vol VIII, 141

There was a water passage ten feet wide, where the river had risen beyond the edge of the ice, but not more than four or five feet was clear of the bushes and trees. By the side of Fair Haven Pond it was particularly narrow. I shoved the ice on the one hand and the bushes and trees on the other all the way. Nor was the passage much wider below, as far back as where I had taken my boat. For all this distance, the river for the most part, as well as all the pond, was an unbroken field of ice. I went winding my way and scraping between the maples. Half a dozen rods off on the ice, you would not have supposed that there was room for a boat there. In some places you could have got on to the ice from the shore without much difficulty.

8 April, 1856, Journal Vol VIII, 259

I set out to sail, the wind northwest, but it is so strong, and I so feeble, that I gave it up. The waves dashed over into the boat and with their sprinkling wet me half through in a few moments. Our meadow looks as angry now as it ever can.

10 April, 1856, Journal Vol VIII, 271

I steer down straight through the Great Meadows, with the wind almost directly aft, feeling it more and more the farther I advance into them. They make a noble lake now. The boat, tossed up by the rolling billows, keeps falling again on the waves with a chucking sound which is inspiriting.

14 April, 1856, Journal Vol VIII, 282

Now comes the rain with a rush. In haste I put my boat about, raise my sail, and, cowering under my umbrella in the stern, with the steering oar in my hand, begin to move homeward. The rain soon fulls up my sail, and it catches all the little wind. From under the umbrella I look out on the scene. The big drops pepper the water plain, the aequor, on every side. It is not a hard, dry pattering, as on a roof, but a softer, liquid pattering, which makes the impression of a double wateriness. You do not observe the drops descending but where they strike, for there they batter and indent the surface deeply like buckshot, and they, or else other drops which they create, rebound or hop up an inch or two, and these last you see, and also when they fall back broken into small shot and roll on the surface. Around each shot-mark are countless circling dimples, running into and breaking one another, and very often a bubble is formed by the force of the shot, which float entire for half a minute. These big shot are battering the surface every three inches or thicker, I make haste to take down my sail at the bridges, but at the stone arches forgot my umbrella, which was unavoidably crushed in part. Even in the midst of this rain I am struck by the variegated surface of the water, different portions reflecting the light differently, giving what is called a watered appearance. Broad streams of light water stretch away between streams of dark, as if they were different kinds of water unwilling to mingle, though all are equally dimpled by the rain, and you detect no difference in their condition. As if Nature loved variety for its own sake. It is a true April shower, or rain, —I think the first. It rains so easy, —has a genius for it and infinite capacity for [it]. Many showers will not exhaust the moisture of April.

17 April, 1856, Journal Vol VIII, 290-291

Do not sail well till I reach Dove Rock, then glide swiftly up the stream. I move upward against the current with a moderate but fair wind, the waves somewhat larger, probably because the wind contends with the current. The sun is in my face, and the waves look particularly lively and sparkling. I can steer and write at the same time. They gurgle under my stern, in haste to fill the hollow which I have created. The waves seem to leap and roll like porpoises, with a slight surging sound when their crests break, and I feel an agreeable sense that I am swiftly gliding over and through them, bound on my own errands, while their motion is chiefly but an undulation, and an apparent one. It is pleasant, exhilarating, to feel the boat tossed up a little by them from time to time. Perhaps a wine-drinker would say it was like the effect of wine. It is flattering to a sense of power to make the wayward wind our horse and sit with our hand on the tiller. Sailing is much like flying, and from the birth of our race men have been charmed by it.

29 April, 1856, Journal Vol VIII, 317

Take my first skate to Fair Haven Pond.

It takes my feet a few moments to get used to the skates. I see the track of one skater who has preceded me this morning. This is the first skating. I keep mostly to the smooth ice about a rod wide next the shore commonly, where there was an overflow a day or two ago. There is not the slightest overflow to-day, and yet it is warm (thermometer at 25 at 4:30 P.M.). It must be that the river is falling. Now I go shaking over hobbly places, now shoot over a bridge of ice only a foot wide between the water and the shore at a bend, —Hubbard Bath, —always so at first there. Now I suddenly see the trembling surface of water where I thought were black spots of ice only around me. The river is rather low, so that I cannot keep the river above the Clamshell Bend. I am confined to a very narrow edging of ice in the meadow, gliding with unexpected ease through withered sedge, but slipping sometimes on a twig; again taking to the snow to reach the next ice, but this rests my feet; straddling the bare black willows, winding between the button-bushes, and following narrow threadings of ice amid the sedge, which bring me out to clear fields unexpectedly. Occasionally I am obliged to take a few strokes over black and thin-looking ice, where the neighboring bank is springy, and am slow to acquire confidence in it, but, returning, how bold I am! Where the meadow seemed only sedge and snow, I find a complete ice connection.

At Cardinal Shore, as usual, there is a great crescent of hobbly ice, where, two or three days ago, the northwest wind drove the waves back up-stream and broke up the edge of the ice. This crescent is eight or ten rods wide and twice as many long, and consists of cakes of ice from a few inches to half a dozen feet in diameter, with each a raised edge all around, where apparently the floating sludge has been caught and accumulated. (Occasionally the raised edge is six inches high!) This is mottled black and white, and is not yet safe. It is like skating over so many rails, or the edges of saws. Now I glide over a field of white air-cells close to the surface, with coverings no thicker than egg-shells, cutting through with a sharp crackling sound. There are many of those singular spider-shaped dark places amid the white ice, where the surface water has run through some days ago.

7 December, 1856, Journal Vol IX, 165-167

Walden froze completely over last night. This is very sudden, for on the evening of the 15th there was not a particle of ice in it. In just three days, then, it has been completely frozen over, and the ice is now from two and a half to three inches thick, a transparent green ice, through which I see the bottom where it is seven or eight feet deep. I detect its thickness by looking at the cracks, which are already very numerous, but, having been made at different stages of the ice, they indicate very various thicknesses. Often one only an inch deep crosses at right angles another two and a half inches deep, the last having been recently made and indicating the real thickness of the ice. I advance confidently toward the middle, keeping within a few feet of some distinct crack two inches or more deep, but when that fails me and I see only cracks an inch or an inch and a half deep, or none at all, I walk with great caution and timidity, though the ice may be as thick as ever, but I have no longer the means of determining its thickness. The ice is so transparent that it is too much like walking on water by faith.

19 December, 1856, Journal Vol IX, 189-190

When I turn about, it requires all my strength and skill to push the boat back again. I must keep it pointed directly in the teeth of the wind. If it turns a little, the wind gets the advantage of me and I lose ground. The wind being against the stream makes it rise the faster, and also prevents the driftwood from coming down. How many a meadow my boat's bottom has rubbed over! I might perhaps consult with it respecting cranberry vines, cut-grass, pitcher-plant, etc., etc.

27 October, 1857, Journal Vol IX, 130

It is a strong but fitful northwest wind, stronger than before. Under my new sail, the boat dashes off like a horse with the bits in his teeth. Coming into the main stream below the island, a sudden flaw strikes me, and in my efforts to keep the channel I run one side under, and so am compelled to beach my boat there and bail it.

23 August, 1858, Journal Vol XI, 120

As I am paddling home swiftly before the northwest wind, absorbed in my wooding, I see, this cool and grayish evening, that peculiar yellow light in the east, from the sun a little before its setting. It has just come out beneath a great cold slate-colored cloud that occupies most of the western sky, as smaller ones the eastern, and now its rays, slanting over the hill in whose shadow I float, fall on the eastern trees and hills with a thin yellow light like a clear yellow wine, but somehow it reminds me that now the hearth-side is getting to be a more comfortable place than out-of-doors.

21 October, 1858, Journal Vol X, 115

I sailed swiftly, standing up and tipping my boat to make a keel of its side, though at first it was hard to keep off a lee shore. I looked for cranberries drifted up on the lee side of the meadows, but saw few. It was exciting to feel myself tossed by the dark waves and hear them surge about me. The reign of water now begins, and how it gambols and revels! Waves are its leaves, foam its blossoms. How they run and leap in great droves, deriving new excitement from each other! Schools of porpoises and blackfish are only more animated waves and have acquired the gait and game of the sea itself. The high wind and the dashing waves are very inspiriting.

27 October, 1858, Journal Vol X, 130

Paddle round Beaver Pond in a boat, which I calked with newspaper. It has a very boggy and generally inaccessible shore, now more inaccessible than usual on account of the rain and high water. A singularly muddy hole.

17 September, 1858, Journal Vol XI, 162

I walk about the pond looking at the shores, since I have not paddled about it much of late years. What a grand place for a promenade!

28 December, 1858, Journal Vol XI, 380

I think more of skates than of the horse or locomotive as annihilators of distance, for while I am getting along with the speed of the horse, I have at the same time the satisfaction of the horse and his rider, and far more adventure and variety than if I were riding. We never cease to be surprised when we observe how swiftly the skater glides along. Just compare him with one walking or running. The walker is but a snail in comparison, and the runner gives up the contest after a few rods. The skater can afford to follow all the windings of a stream, and yet soon leaves far behind and out of sight the walker who cuts across. Distance is hardly an obstacle to him. . . . The new stroke is eighteen or twenty inches one side of the old. The briskest walkers appear to be stationary to the skater. The skater has wings, talaria, to his feet. Moreover, you have such perfect control of your feet that you can take advantage of the narrowest and most winding and sloping bridge of ice in order to pass between the button-bushes and the open stream or under a bridge on a narrow shelf, where the walker cannot go at all. You can glide securely within an inch of destruction on this the most slippery of surfaces, more securely than you could walk there, perhaps, on any other material. You can pursue swiftly the most intricate and winding path, even leaping obstacles which suddenly present themselves.

29 December, 1858, Journal Vol XI, 381-382

The river, now that it is so clear and sunny, is better than any aquarium. Standing up and pushing gently up the stream, or floating yet more quietly down it, I can, in some places, see the secrets of half the river and its inhabitants.

8 August, 1859, Journal Vol XII, 280

Rice has had a little experience once in pushing a canal-boat up Concord River. Says this was the way they used to get the boat off a rock when by chance it had got on to one. If it had run quite on, so that the rock was partly under the main bottom of the boat, they let the boat swing round to one side and placed a stout stake underneath, a little aslant, with one end on the bottom of the river and the other ready to catch the bows of the boat, and while one held it, perhaps, the other pushed the boat round again with all his force, and so drove it on to the stake and lifted it up above the rock, and so it floated off.

8 August, 1859, Journal Vol XII, 281

How many memorable localities in a river walk! Here is the warm wood-side; next, the good fishing bay; and next, where the old settler was drowned when crossing on the ice a hundred years ago. It is all storied.

27 January, 1860, Journal Vol XIII, 56

No finer walking in any respect than on our broad meadow highway in the winter, when covered with bare ice. If the ice is wet, you slip in rubbers; but when it is dry and cold, rubbers give you a firm hold, and you walk with a firm and elastic step. I do not know of any more exhilarating walking than up or down a broad field of smooth ice like this in a cold, glittering winter day when your rubbers give you a firm hold on the ice.

10 February, 1860, Journal Vol XIII, 135

The river is rapidly falling, is more than a foot lower than it was a few days ago, so that there is an ice-belt left where the bank is steep, and on this I skate in many places; in others the ice slants from the shore for a rod or two to the water; and on the meadows for the most part there is not water under the ice, and it accordingly rumbles loudly as I go over it, and I rise and fall as I pass over hillocks or hollows.

15 February, 1860, Journal Vol XIII, 146

When, as was commonly the case, I had none to commune with, I used to raise the echoes by striking with a paddle on the side of my boat, filling the surrounding woods with circling and dilating sound, stirring them up as the keeper of a menagerie his wild beasts, until I elicited a growl from every wooded vale and hill-side.

Walden, 113

By the way there came up a shower, which compelled me to stand half an hour under a pine, piling boughs over my head, and wearing my handkerchief for a shed; and when at length I had made one cast over the pickerel-weed, standing up to my middle in water, I found myself suddenly in the shadow of a cloud, and the thunder began to rumble with such emphasis that I could do no more than listen to it. The gods must be proud, thought I, with such forked flashes to rout a poor unarmed fisherman. So I made haste for shelter to the nearest hut, which stood half a mile from any road, but so much the nearer to the pond, and had long been uninhabited.

Walden, 132

As I was paddling along the north shore on very calm October afternoon, for such days especially they settle on to the lakes, like the milkweed down, having looked in vain over the pond for a loon, suddenly one, sailing out from the shore toward the middle a few rods in front of me, set up his wild laugh and betrayed himself. I pursued with a paddle and he dived, but when he came up I was nearer than before. He dived again, but I miscalculated the direction he would take, and we were fifty rods apart when he came to the surface this time, for I had helped to widen the interval; and again he laughed long and loud, and with more reason than before. He manoeuvred so cunningly that I could not get within half a dozen rods of him. Each time, when he came to the surface, turning his head this way and that, he coolly surveyed the water and the land, and apparently chose his course so that he might come up where there was the widest expanse of water and at the greatest distance from the boat. It was surprising how quickly he made up his mind and put his resolve into execution. He led me at once to the widest part of the pond, and could not be driven from it. While he was thinking one thing in his brain, I was endeavoring to divine his thought in mine. It was a pretty game, played on the smooth surface of the pond, a man against a loon. Suddenly your adversary's checker disappears beneath the board, and the problem is to place yours nearest to where his will appear again. Sometimes he would come up unexpectedly on the opposite side of me, having apparently passed directly under the boat. So long-winded was he and so unweariable, that when he had swum farthest he would immediately plunge again, nevertheless; and then no wit could divine where in the deep pond, beneath the smooth surface, he might be speeding his way like a fish, for he had time and ability to visit the bottom of the pond in its deepest part. It is said that loons have been caught in New York lakes eighty feet beneath the surface, with hooks set for trout, —though Walden is deeper than that. How surprised must the fishes be to see this ungainly visitor from another sphere speeding his way amid their schools! Yet he appeared to know his course as surely under water as on the surface, and swam much faster there. Once or twice I saw a ripple where he approached the surface, just put his head out to reconnoitre, and instantly dived again. I found that it was as well for me to rest on my oars and wait his reappearing as to endeavor to calculate where he would rise; for again and again, when I was straining my eyes over the surface one way, I would suddenly be startled by his unearthly laugh behind me. But why, after displaying so much cunning did he invariably betray himself the moment he came up by the loud laugh? Did not his white breast enough betray him? He was indeed a silly loon, I thought. I could commonly hear the plash of the water when he came up, and so also detected him. But after an hour he seemed as fresh as ever, dived as willingly and swam yet farther than at first. It was surprising to see how serenely he sailed off with unruffled breast when he came to the surface, doing all the work with his webbed feet beneath. His usual note was this demoniac laughter, yet somewhat like that of a water-fowl; but occasionally, when he had balked me most successfully and come up a long way off, he uttered a long-drawn unearthly howl, probably more like that of a wolf than any bird; as when a beast puts his muzzle to the ground and deliberately howls. This was his looning, —perhaps the wildest sound that is ever heard here, making the woods ring far and wide. I concluded that he laughed in derision of my efforts, confident of his own resources. Though the sky was by this time overcast, the pond was so smooth that I could see where he broke the surface when I did not hear him. His white breast, the stillness of the air, and the smoothness of the water were all against him. At length, having come up fifty rods off, he uttered one of those prolonged howls, as if calling on the god of loons to aid him, and immediately there came a wind from the east and rippled the surface, and filled the whole air with misty rain, and I was impressed as if it were the prayer of the loon answered, and his god was angry with me; and so I left him disappearing far away on the tumultuous surface.

Walden, 152-153

As we thus dipped our way along between fresh masses of foliage overrun with the grape and smaller flowering vines, the surface was so calm, and both air and water so transparent, that the flight of a kingfisher or robin over the river was as distinctly seen reflected in the water below as in the air above. The birds seemed to flit through submerged groves, alighting on the yielding sprays, and their clear notes to come up from below. We were uncertain whether the water floated the land, or the land held the water in its bosom.

A Week, 49-50

The north wind stepped readily into the harness which we had provided, and pulled us along with good will. Sometimes we sailed as gently and steadily as the clouds overhead, watching the receding shores and the motions of our sail; the play of its pulse so like our own lives, so thin and yet so full of life, so noiseless when it labored hardest, so noisy and impatient when least effective; now bending to some generous impulse of the breeze, and then fluttering and flapping with a kind of human suspense. It was the scale on which the varying temperature of distant atmospheres was graduated, and it was some attraction for use that the breeze it played with had been out of doors so long. Thus we sailed, not being able to fly, but as next best, making a long furrow in the fields of the Merrimack toward our home, with our wings spread, but never lifting our heel from the watery trench; gracefully plowing homeward with our brisk and willing team, wind and stream, pulling together, the former yet a wild steer, yoked to his more sedate fellow. It was very near flying, as when the duck rushes through the water with an impulse of her wings, throwing the spray about her, before she can rise.

A Week, 450-451

We were soon in the smooth water of the Quakish Lake, and took our turns at rowing and paddling across it. It is a small, irregular, but handsome lake, shut in on all sides by the forest, and showing no traces of man but some low boom in a distant cove, reserved for spring use.

The Maine Woods, 33

In the night I dreamed of trout-fishing; and, when at length I awoke, it seemed a fable, that this painted fish swam there so near my couch, and rose to our hooks the last evening—and I doubted if I had not dreamed it all. So I arose before dawn to test its truth, while my companions were still sleeping. There stood Ktaadn with distinct and cloudless outline in the moonlight; and the rippling of the rapids was the only sound to break the stillness. Standing on the shore, I once more cast my line into the stream, and found the dream to be real, and the fable true. The speckled trout and silvery roach, like flying fish, sped swiftly through the moonlight air, describing bright arcs on the dark side of Ktaadn, until moonlight, now fading into daylight, brought satiety to my mind, and the minds of my companions, who had joined me.

The Maine Woods, 55

The stream was only from one and one half to three rods wide, quite winding, with occasional small islands, meadows, and some very swift and shallow places. When we came to an island, the Indian never hesitated which side to take, as if the current told him which was the shortest and deepest. It was lucky for us that the water was so high. We had to walk but once on this stream, carrying a part of the load, at a swift and shallow reach, while he got up with the canoe, not being obliged to take out, though he said it was very strong water.

The Maine Woods, 210

Though the bay in which we were was perfectly quiet and smooth, we found the lake already wide awake outside, but not dangerously or unpleasantly so; nevertheless, when you get out on one of those lakes in a canoe like this, you do not forget that you are completely at the mercy of the wind, and a fickle power it is. The playful waves may at any time become too rude for you in their sport, and play right on over you.

The Maine Woods, 241

The morning was a bright one and perfectly still and serene, the lake as smooth as glass, we making the only ripples as we paddled into it.

The Maine Woods, 264

He had previously complimented me on my paddling, saying that I paddled "just like anybody," giving me an Indian name which meant "great paddler." When off this stream he said to me, who sat in the bows, "Me teach you paddle." So turning toward the shore he got out, came forward and placed my hands as he wished. He placed one of them quite outside the boat, and the other parallel with the first, grasping the paddle near the end, not over the flat extremity, and told me to slide it back and forth on the side of the canoe. This, I found, was a great improvement which I had not thought of, saving me the labor of lifting the paddle each time, and I wondered that he had not suggested it before. It is true, before our baggage was reduced we had been obliged to sit with our legs drawn up, and our knees above the side of the canoe, which would have prevented our paddling thus, or perhaps he was afraid of wearing out his canoe, by constant friction on the side.

I told him that I had been accustomed to sit in the stern, and lifting my paddle at each stroke, getting a pry on the side each time, and I still paddled partly as if in the stern. He then wanted to see me paddle in the stern. So, changing paddles, for he had the longer and better one, and turning end for end, he sitting flat on the bottom and I on the crossbar, he began to paddle very hard, trying to turn the canoe, looking over his shoulder and laughing, but finding it in vain he relaxed his efforts, though we still sped along a mile or two very swiftly. He said that he had no fault to find with my paddling in the stern, but I complained that he did not paddle according to his own directions in the bows.

The Maine Woods, 295-296

I have not yet found a new jacknife but I had a glorious skating with Channing the other day on the skates found long ago.

6 January, 1855, Correspondence, 362

You should have been here to help me get in my boat. The last time I used it, November 27th, paddling up the Assabet, I saw a great round log sunk deep in the water, and with labor got it aboard. When I was floating this home so gently, it occurred to me why I had found it. It was to make wheels with to roll my boat into the winter quarters upon. As I sawed off two thick rollers from one end, pierced them for wheels, and then of a joist I had found drifting on the river in the summer I made an axletree, and on this I rolled my boat out.

9 December, 1855, Correspondence, 400

Now I forgot that I had been wetted, and wanted to embrace and mingle myself with the water.

I lie almost flat, resting my hands on what offers, to drink at this water where it bubbles, at the very udders of Nature, for man is never weaned from her breast while this life lasts.

Contact

MUCH OF THOREAU'S daily life was spent trying to come into as close contact as possible with the world around him, and in so doing, recover a sense of the vital force pumping through himself as it did through all nature. He fulfilled this goal by boating, skating, swimming, and sometimes even crawling on his belly in shallows. "We need the tonic of wilderness—to wade sometimes in meadows where only the bittern and meadow-hen lurk," he claimed.

For Thoreau, bathing and swimming, especially in Walden Pond, was a form of spiritual baptism, reconnecting his soul to that of nature in a kind of spiritual water dance. Here, by renewing his original communion with nature, and in so doing, rejuvenating his own health, Thoreau could satisfy his long held desire to blend his mystical life with that of his primitive savage life: "When I would recreate myself, I seek . . . the thickest and most interminable and, to the citizen, most dismal swamp. I enter a swamp as a sacred place, a sanctum sanatorium. There is the strength, the marrow of nature."

Thoreau ever struggled to find ways to link nature's wildness with his own, and by immersing himself directly in water he could achieve the physical redemption of his absolute potential. "That part of you that is wettest is fullest of life," he once stated. With spray blowing into his face, Thoreau felt himself anointed by nature's blessing in an act of ritual, which, like that of bathing, was a form of what he referred to as "sensuous immersion." Full bodily contact with water was, for Thoreau, possibly as erotic an experience as he could imagine.

Thoreau was happiest when he was wettest, taking every opportunity to drink the ambrosial fluid of nature, not just through direct ingestion but also through bodily assimilation. Walking along Cape Cod, he rejoiced in the feel of the sea in the air about him, complaining only that he could not seem to get enough of the ocean into him. Wading along rivers, Thoreau rejoiced in the touch of the water and found it "delicious" to let his "legs drink" as he took his river walks "endwise." Once, while in Maine, Thoreau wandered off the trail and spent an entire afternoon bush-crashing and wading through a series of wetlands. When asked why he didn't just follow the leader's track, Thoreau countered that he "would not have missed that walk for a good deal."

Ever the melancholic, Hawthorne once wrote that: "Walden Pond is clear and beautiful, as usual. It tempted me to bathe; and though the water was thrillingly cold, it was like the thrill of a happy death." It is bittersweet to recount that Thoreau went swimming in the Mississippi during his last trip taken to cure himself of the disease that would later claim him. Did he think back, one wonders, to his previous pleasures of engaging in the sensuous luxury of such bathing? —"to feel the wind blow on your body, the water flow on you and love you, is a rare enjoyment."

Would it not be a luxury to stand up to one's chin in some retired swamp for a whole summer's day, scenting the sweet-fern and bilberry blows, and lulled by the minstrelsy of gnats and mosquitoes? A day passed in the society of those Greek sages, such as described in the "Banquet" of Xenophon, would not be comparable with the dry wit of decayed cranberry vines, and the fresh Attic salt of the moss beds. Say twelve hours of genial and familiar converse with the leopard frog. The sun to rise behind alder and dogwood, and climb buoyantly to his meridian of three hands' breadth, and finally sink to rest behind some bold western hummock. To hear the evening chant of the mosquito from a thousand green chapels, and the bittern begin to boom from his concealed fort like a sunset gun! Surely, one may as profitably be soaked in the juices of a marsh for one day, as pick his way dry-shod over sand. Cold and damp, —are they not as rich experience as warmth and dryness?

16 June, 1840, Journal Vol I, 141-142

My companion said he would drink when the boat got under the bridge, because the water would be cooler in the shade, though the stream quickly passes through the piers from shade to sun again. It is something beautiful, that act of drinking, the stooping to imbibe some of the widespread element, in obedience to instinct, without whim. We do no so simply drink in other influences. It is pleasant to have been to a place by the way a river went.

19 September, 1850, Journal Vol II, 71

I am on my way to the river behind Hubbard's to bathe. After hoeing in a dusty garden all this warm afternoon, so warm that the baker says he never knew the like and expects to find his horses dead in the stable when he gets home, —it is very grateful to wend one's way at evening to some pure and cool stream and bathe therein.

30 June, 1851, Journal Vol II, 277

I bathe me in the river. I lie down were it is shallow, amid the weeds over its sandy bottom; but it seems shrunken and parched; I find it difficult to get wet through. I would fain be the channel of a mountain brook. I bathe, and in a few hours I bathe again, not remembering that I was wetted before. When I come to the river, I take off my clothes and carry them over, then bathe and wash off the mud and continue my walk.

22 July, 1851, Journal Vol II, 335

Full moon. Arose and went to the river and bathed, stepping very carefully not to disturb the household, and still carefully in the street not to disturb the neighbors. I did not walk naturally and freely till I had got over the wall. Then to Hubbard's Bridge at 2 A.M.

12 August, 1851, Journal Vol II, 383

To Walden to bathe at 5:30 A.M.

23 August, 1851, Journal Vol II, 419

I had already bathed in Walden as I passed, but now I forgot that I had been wetted, and wanted to embrace and mingle myself with the water of Flint's Pond this warm afternoon, to get wet inwardly and deeply.

12 September, 1851, Journal Vol II, 501

Both air and water are so transparent that the fisherman tries in vain to deceive the fish with his baits. Even our commonly muddy river looks clear to-day. I find the water suddenly cold, and that the bathing days are over.

25 September, 1851, Journal Vol III, 21-22

Sitting by Spruce swamp in Contant's Grove, I am reminded that this is a perfect day to visit the swamps, with its damp, mistling, mildewy air, so solemnly still.

28 September, 1851, Journal Vol III, 33

Though the moss is comparatively dry, I cannot walk without upsetting the numerous pitchers, which are now full of water, and so wetting my feet. I once accidentally sat down on such a bed of pitcher-plants, and found an uncommonly wet seat where I expected a dry one.

28 September, 1851, Journal Vol III, 33

Men are inclined to be amphibious, to sympathize with fishes, now. I desire to get wet and saturated with water. The North River, Assabet, by the old stone bridge, affords the best bathing-place I think of, —a grassy bank, and overhanging maples, with transparent water, deep enough, where you can see every fish in it. Though you stand still, you feel the rippling current about you.

15 June, 1852, Journal Vol IV, 100

Walden imparts to the body of the bather a remarkably chalky-white appearance, whiter than natural, tinged with blue, which, combined with its magnifying and distorting influence, produces a monstrous and ogre-like effect, proving, nevertheless, the purity of the water. The river water, on the other hand, imparts to the bather a yellowish tinge.

28 June, 1852, Journal Vol IV, 160

How cheering it is to behold a full spring bursting forth directly from the earth, like this of Tarbell's, from clean gravel, copiously, in a thin sheet; for it descends at once, where you see no opening, cool from the caverns of the earth, and making a considerable stream. Such springs, in the sale of the lands, are not valued for as much as they are worth. I lie almost flat, resting my hands on what offers, to drink at this water where it bubbles, at the very udders of Nature, for man is never weaned from her breast while this life lasts. How many times in a single walk does he stoop for a draught!

5 July, 1852, Journal Vol IV, 188

We undressed on this side, carried our clothes down in the stream a considerable distance, and finally bathed in earnest from the opposite side. The heat tempted us to prolong this luxury. I think that I never felt the water so warm, yet it was not disagreeably so, though probably bathing in [it] was the less bracing and exhilarating, not so good as when you have to make haste, shivering, to get your clothes on in the wind; when ice has formed in the morning. But this is certainly the most luxurious. The river has here a sandy bottom and is for the most part quite shallow. I made quite an excursion up and down it in the water, a fluvial, a water, walk. It seemed the properest highway for this weather. Now in water a foot or two deep, now suddenly descending through valleys up to my neck, but all alike agreeable. Sometimes the bottom looked as if covered with long, flat, sharp-edged rocks. I could break off cakes three or four inches thick and a foot or two square. It was a conglomeration and consolidation of sand and pebbles, as it were cemented to the depth of an inch on the upper side, - a hard kind of pan covering or forming the bottom in many places. When I had left the river and walked in the woods for some time, and jumped into the river again, I was surprised to find for the first time how warm it was, —as it seemed to me, almost warm enough to boil eggs, —like water that has stood a considerable while in a kettle over a fire. There are many interesting objects of study as you walk up and down a clear river like this in the water, where you can see every inequality in the bottom and every object on it.

10 July, 1852, Journal Vol IV, 211-212

I wonder if any Roman emperor ever indulged in such luxury as this, —of walking up and down a river in torrid weather with only a hat to shade the head. What were the baths of Caracalla to this? Now we traverse a long water plain some two feet deep; now we descend into a darker river valley, where the bottom is lost sight of and the water rises to our armpits; now we go over a hard iron pan; now we stoop and go under a low bough of the *Salix nigra*; now we slump into soft mud amid the pads of the *Nympoea odorata*, at this hour shut. On this road there is not other traveller to turn out for.

10 July, 1852, Journal Vol IV, 214

Now for another fluvial walk. There is always a current of air above the water, blowing up or down the course of the river, so that this is the coolest highway. Divesting yourself of all clothing but your shirt and hat, which are to protect your exposed parts from the sun, you are prepared for the fluvial excursion. You choose what depths you like, tucking your toga higher or lower, as you take the deep middle of the road or the shallow sidewalks. Here is a road where no dust was ever known, no tolerable drouth. Now your feet expand on a smooth sandy bottom, now contract timidly on pebbles, now slump in genial fatty mud—greasy, saponaceous—amid the pads. You scare out whole schools of small beams and perch, and sometimes a pickerel, which have taken shelter from the sun under the pads. This river is so clear compared with the South Branch, or main stream, that all their secrets are betrayed to you. Or you meet with and interrupt a turtle taking a more leisurely walk up the stream. Ever and anon you cross some furrow in the sand, made by a muskrat, leading off to right or left to their galleries in the bank, and you thrust your foot into the entrance, which is just below the surface of the water and is strewn with grass and rushes, of which they make their nests. In shallow water near the shore, your feet at once detect the presence of springs in the bank emptying in, by the sudden coldness of the water, and there, if you are thirsty, you dig a little well in the sand with your hands, and when you return, after it has settled and clarified itself, get a draught of pure cold water there.

12 July, 1852, Journal Vol IV, 220-221

I find, on bathing, that the water has been made very cold by the rain-storm, so that I soon come out. It must affect the fishes very much.

31 August, 1852, Journal Vol IV, 328-329

When I have left the boat a short time the seats become intoler-ably hot. What a luxury to bathe now! It is gloriously hot, —the first of this weather. I cannot get wet enough. I must let the water soak into me. When you come out, it is rapidly dried on you or absorbed into your body, and you want to go in again. I begin to inhabit the planet, and see how I may be naturalized at last.

3 July, 1854, Journal Vol V, 382-283

Took my last bath the 24th. Probably shall not bathe again this year. It was chilling cold.

26 September, 1854, Journal Vol VII, 58

My seat from time to time is the springy horizontal bough of some fallen tree which is frozen into the ice, some old maple that had blown over and retained some life for a year after in the water, covered with the great shaggy perforate parmelia. Lying flat, I quench my thirst where it is melted about it, blowing aside the snow-fleas.

1 February, 1855, Journal Vol VII, 161-162

Bathing in Walden, I find the water considerably colder at the bottom while I stand up to my chin, but the sandy bottom much warmer to my feet than the water. The heat passes through the water with[out] being absorbed by it much.

23 July, 1855, Journal Vol VIII, 424

I enjoy more drinking water at a clear spring than out of a goblet at a gentleman's table.

20 October, 1855, Journal Vol VII, 503

At length, when the river turned more easterly, I was obliged to take down my sail and paddle slowly in the face of the rain, for the most part not seeing my course, with the umbrella slanted before me. But though my progress was slow and laborious, and at length I began to get a little wet, I enjoyed the adventure because it combined to some extent the advantages of being at home in my chamber and abroad in the storm at the same time.

22 April, 1856, Journal Vol VIII, 299

Lunched by the spring on the Brady farm in Freetown, and there it occurred to me how to get clear water from a spring when the surface is covered with dust or insects. Thrust your dipper down deep in the middle of the spring and lift it up quickly straight and square. This will heap up the water in the middle so that the scum will run off.

24 June, 1856, Journal Vol VIII, 385

I go up the river as far as Hubbard's Second Grove, in order to share the general commotion and excitement of the elements, —wind and waves and rain.

27 October, 1858, Journal Vol X, 129

I see stretching from side to side of the smooth brook, where it is three or four feet wide, apparently an invisible waving line like a cobweb, against which the water is heaped up a very little. This line is constantly swayed to and fro, as by the current or wind bellying forward here and there. I try repeatedly to catch and break it with my hand and let the water run free, but still, to my surprise, I clutch nothing but fluid, and the imaginary line keeps its place. Is it the fluctuating edge of a lighter, perhaps more oily, fluid, overflowing a heavier? I see several such lines. It is somewhat like the slightest conceivable smoothfall over a dam. I must ask the water-bug that glides across it.

24 January, 1858, Journal Vol X, 256

What a contrast to sink your head so as to cover your ears with water, and hear only the confused noise of the rushing river, and then to raise your ears above water and hear the steady creaking of crickets in the aerial universe!

7 September, 1858, Journal Vol XI, 150

For refreshment on these voyages, [we] are compelled to drink the warm and muddy-tasted river water out of a clamshell which we keep, —so that it reminds you of a clam soup, —taking many a sup, or else leaning over the side of the boat while the other leans the other way to keep your balance, and often plunging your whole face in at that, when the oar dips or the waves run.

31 July, 1859, Journal Vol XII, 268

The best way to drink, especially at a shallow spring, or one so sunken below the surface as to be difficult to reach, is through a tube. You can commonly find growing near a spring a hollow reed or weed of some kind suitable for this purpose, such as rue or touch-me-not or water saxifrage, or you can carry one in your pocket.

12 July, 1860, Journal Vol XIII, 398

This afternoon, again walked to the larger northeast swamp, going directly, i.e. east of the promonotories or part way down the slopes. Bathed in the small rocky basin above the smaller meadow. These two swamps are about the wildest part of the mountain and most interesting to me. The smaller occurs on the northeast side of the main mountain, i.e. at the northwest end of the plateau. It is a little roundish meadow a few rods over, with cotton-grass in it, the shallow bottom of a basin of rock, and out the east side there trickles a very slight stream, just moistening the rock at present and collecting enough in one cavity to afford you a drink.

6 August, 1860, Journal Vol VIV, 17-18

Water stands in shallow pools on almost every rocky shelf. The largest pool of open water which I found was on the southwest side of the summit, and was four rods long by fifteen to twenty feet in width and a foot deep. Wool- and cotton-grass grew around it, and there was a dark green moss and some mud at the bottom. There was a smoother similar pool on the next shelf above it. These were about the same size in June and in August, and apparently never dry up. There was also the one in which I bathed, near the northeast little meadow. I had a delicious bath there, though the water was warm, but there was a pleasant strong and drying wind blowing over the ridge, and when I had bathed, the rock felt like plush to my feet.

9 August, 1860, Journal Vol VIV, 45-46

Commonly I rested an hour or two in the shade at noon, after planting, and ate my lunch, and read a little by a spring which was the source of a swamp and of a brook, oozing from under Brister's Hill, half a mile from my field. The approach to this was through a succession of descending grassy hollows, full of young pitch-pines, into a larger wood about the swamp. There, in a very secluded and shaded spot, under a spreading white-pine, there was yet a clean firm sward to sit on. I had dug out the spring and made a well of clear gray water, where I could dip up a pailful without roiling it, and thither I went for this purpose almost every day in midsummer, when the pond was warmest.

Walden, 147-148

All the morning we had heard the sea roar on the eastern shore, which was several miles distant; for it still felt the effects of the storm in which the St. John was wrecked, - though a school-boy, whom we overtook, hardly knew what we meant, his ears were so used to it. He would have more plainly heard the same sound in a shell. It was a very inspiring sound to walk by, filling the whole air, that of the sea dashing against the land, heard several mile inland. Instead of having a dog to growl before your door, to have an Atlantic Ocean to growl for a whole Cape! On the whole, we were glad of the storm, which would show us the ocean in its angriest mood.

Cape Cod, 45-46

Though for some time I have not spoken of the roaring of the breakers, and the ceaseless flux and reflux of the waves, yet they did not for a moment cease to dash and roar, with such a tumult that if you had been there, you could scarcely have heard my voice the while; and they are dashing and roaring this very moment, though it may be with less din and violence, for there the sea never rests. We were wholly absorbed by this spectacle and tumult, and like Chryses, though in a different mood from him, we walked silent along the shore of the resounding sea.

Cape Cod, 76

Though we have indulged in some placid reflections of late, the reader must not forget that the dash and roar of the waves were incessant. Indeed, it would be well if he were to read with a large conch-shell at his ear.

Cape Cod, 147

Again we took to a beach for another day (October 13), walking along the shore of the resounding sea, determined to get it into us.

Cape Cod, 206

From time to time we lay down and drank at little pools in the sand, filled with pure fresh water, all that was left, probably, of a pond or swamp.

Cape Cod, 238

We thus travelled about four miles in the very torrent itself, continually crossing and recrossing it, leaping from rock to rock, and jumping with the stream down falls of seven or eight feet, or sometimes sliding down on our backs in a thin sheet of water.

The Maine Woods, 67

The cool air above, and the continual bathing of our bodies in mountain water, alternate foot, sitz, douche, and plunge bathes, made this walk exceedingly refreshing, and we had travelled only a mile or two after leaving the torrent, before every thread of our clothes was as dry as usual, owing perhaps to a peculiar quality in the atmosphere.

The Maine Woods, 68

The stream, though narrow and swift, was still deep, with a muddy bottom, as I proved by diving to it.

The Maine Woods, 208-209

We all three walked into the lake up to our middle to wash our clothes.

The Maine Woods, 221

What wholesome herb drinks are to be had in the swamps now! What strong medicinal but rich scents from the decaying leaves! The rain falling on the freshly dried herbs and leaves, and filling the pools and ditches into which they have dropped thus clean and rigid, will soon convert them into tea, —green, black, brown, and yellow teas,of all degrees of strength, enough to set all Nature a-gossiping. Whether we drink them or not, as yet, before their strength is drawn, these leaves, dried on great Nature's coppers, are of such various pure and delicate tints as might make the fame of Oriental teas.

Autumnal Tints, 156

If one would reflect, let him embark on some placid stream, and float with the current.

Drifting in a sultry day on the sluggish waters of the pond, I almost cease to live and begin to be.

Contemplation

Thoreau sought balance between a life of sensations and a life of thought. Not for him, was the sequestered life of an inward-looking mystic, lost in theoretical and ethereal dreams that clouded an appreciation of the external environment. Instead, he wandered—sometimes at a sprinter's pace—along the path of what has been called empirical or phenomenological theology, as a thirsting sensualist immersed in the very marrow of the world.

Thoreau achieved moments of highest spiritual epiphany when drifting in his boat upon the water. It was when floating and meditating in this way that he often achieved the inner peace he so desired, while at the same time as reaching the peak of his abilities as a descriptive writer. No longer being apart from nature, he became absorbed completely and lovingly into her embrace. "I am never so prone to lose my identity," he said at such times. Long hours were spent lying across the seat of his boat "dreaming awake" and sensuously letting himself dissolve into and become one with the cosmos: "Floating in still water, I too am a planet, and have my own orbit, in space, and am no longer a satellite of the earth."

Such union of activity and contemplation inspired and regenerated Thoreau. This process of transcendentalism, whereby the observer achieves insight into higher truths as revealed through the inner workings of nature, provided spiritual sustenance for Thoreau, especially during his early years under the tutorage of Emerson. Water bodies served as mirrors to the soul, whose "liberating and civilizing" expanses "give ample scope and range to our thought."

If one would reflect, let him embark on some placid stream, and float with the current. He cannot resist the Muse. As we ascend the stream, plying the paddle course through the brain. We dream of conflict, power, and grandeur. But turn the prow down stream, and rock, tree, kine, knoll, assuming new and varying positions, as wind and water shift the scene, favor the liquid lapse of thought, far-reaching and sublime, but ever calm and gently undulating.

3 November, 1837, Journal Vol I, 8

My friend tells me he has discovered a new note in nature, which he calls the Ice-Harp. Chancing to throw a handful of pebbles upon the pond where there was an air chamber under the ice, it discoursed a pleasant music to him.

5 December, 1837, Journal Vol I, 14-15

Drifting in a sultry day on the sluggish waters of the pond, I almost cease to live and begin to be. A boatman stretched on the deck of his craft and dallying with the noon would be as apt an emblem of eternity for me as the serpent with his tail in his mouth. I am never so prone to lose my identity. I am dissolved in the haze.

4 April, 1839, Journal Vol I, 75

Up this pleasant stream let's row
For the livelong summer's day,
Sprinkling foam where'er we go
In wreaths as white as driven snow.
Ply the oars! away! away!

Now we glide along the shore,
Chucking lilies as we go,
While the yellow-sanded floor
Doggedly resists the oar,
Like some turtle dull and slow.

Now we stem the middle tide,
Plowing through the deepest soil;
Ridges pile on either side,
While we through the furrow glide,
Reaping bubbles for our toil.

Dew before and drought behind,
Onward all doth seem to fly;
Naught contents the eager mind,
Only rapids now are kind,
Forward are the earth and sky

Sudden music strikes the ear,
Leaking out from yonder bank,
Fit such voyagers to cheer.
Sure there must be Naiads here,
Who have kindly played this prank.

There I know the cunning pack
Where yon self-sufficient rill
All its telltale hath kept back,
Through the meadows held its clack,
And now bubbleth its fill.

Silent flows the parent stream,
And if rocks do lie below
Smothers with her waves the din,
As it were a youthful sin,
Just as still and just as slow.

But this gleeful little rill,
Purling round its storied pebble,
Tinkles to the selfsame tune

From December until June,
Nor doth any drought enfeeble

See the sun behind the willows,
Rising through the golden haze,
How he gleams along the billows,
Their white crests the easy pillows
Of his dew-besprinkled rays

Forward press we to the dawning,
For Aurora leads the way,
Sultry noon and twilight scorning;
In each dewdrop of the morning
Lies the promise of a day.

Rivers from the sun do flow,
Springing with the dewy morn;
Voyageurs 'gainst time do row,
Idle noon nor sunset know,
Ever even the dawn

Since that first "Away! away!"
Many a lengthy league we've rowed,
Still the sparrow on the spray
Hastes to usher in the day
With her simple stanza'd ode.

18 July, 1839, Journal Vol I, 84-86

So with a vigorous shove we launch our boat from the bank, while the flags and bulrushes curtsy a God-speed, and drop silently down the stream. As if we had launched our bark in the sluggish current of our thoughts, and were bound nowhither.

11 June, 1840, Journal Vol I, 136

The river down which we glided for that long afternoon was like a clear drop of dew with the heavens and the landscape reflected in it. And as evening drew on, faint purple clouds began to be reflected in its water, and the cow-bells tinkled louder and more incessantly on the banks, and like shy water-rats we stole along near the shore, looking out for a place to pitch our camp.

16 June, 1840, Journal Vol I, 141

The other day I rowed in my boat a free, even lovely young lady, and, as I plied the oars, she sat in the stern, and there was nothing but she between me and the sky. So might all our lives be picturesque if they were free enough, but mean relations and prejudices intervene to shut out the sky, and we never see a man as simple and distinct as the man-weathercock on a steeple.

19 June, 1840, Journal Vol I, 144

I sailed from Fair Haven last evening as gently and steadily as the clouds sail through the atmosphere. The wind came blowing blithely from the southwest fields, and stepped into the folds of our sail like a winged horse, pulling with a strong and steady impulse. The sail bends gently to the breeze, as swells some generous impulse of the heart, and anon flutters and flaps with a kind of human suspense. I could watch the motions of a sail forever, they are so rich and full of meaning. I watch the play of its pulse, as if it were my own blood beating there. The varying temperature of distant atmospheres is graduated on its scale. It is a free, buoyant creature, the bauble of the heavens and the earth. A gay pastime the air plays with it. If it swells and tugs, it is because the sun lays his windy finger on it. The breeze it plays with has been outdoors so long. So thin is it, and yet so full of life; so noiseless when it labors hardest, so noisy and impatient when least serviceable. So am I blown on by God's breath, so flutter and flap, and fill gently out with the breeze.

30 June, 1840, Journal Vol I, 155

I sit in my boat on Walden, playing the flute this evening, and see the perch, which I seem to have charmed, hovering around me, and the moon travelling over the bottom, which is strewn with the wrecks of the forest, and feel that nothing but the wildest imagination can conceive of the manner of life we are living. Nature is a wizard. The Concord nights are stranger than the Arabian nights.

27 May, 1841, Journal Vol I, 260-261

I sailed on the North River last night with my flute, and my music was a tinkling stream which meandered with the river, and fell from note to note as a brook from rock to rock. I did not hear the strains after they had issued from the flute, but before they were breathed into it, for the original strain precedes the sound by as much as the echo follows after, and the rest is the perquisite of the rocks and trees and beasts. Unpremeditated music is the true gauge which measures the current of our thoughts, the very undertow of our life's stream.

18 August, 1841, Journal Vol I, 271-272

I see yonder some men in a boat, which floats buoyantly amid the reflections of the trees, like a feather poised in mid-air, or a leaf wafted gently from its twig to the water without turning over. They seem very delicately to have availed themselves of the natural laws, and their floating there looks like a beautiful and successful experiment in philosophy.

4 September, 1841, Journal Vol I, 283

Water is so much more fine and sensitive an element than earth. A single boatman passing up or down unavoidably shakes the whole of a wide river, and disturbs its every reflection.

19 September, 1850, Journal Vol II, 71

I used to strike with a paddle on the side of my boat on Walden Pond, filling the surrounding woods with circling and dilating sound, awaking the woods, "stirring them up," as a keeper of a menagerie his lions and tigers, a growl from all. All melody is a sweet echo, as it were coincident with [the] movement of our organs. We wake the echo of the place we are in, its slumbering music.

19 September, 1850, Journal Vol II, 82

I am accustomed to regard the smallest brook with as much interest for the time being as if it were the Orinoco or Mississippi. What is the difference, I would like to know, but mere size? And when a tributary rill empties in, it is like the confluence of famous rivers I have read of. When I cross one on a fence, I love to pause in mid-passage and look down into the water, and study its bottom, its little mystery.

15 November, 1850, Journal Vol II, 96-97

Skated to Sudbury. A beautiful, summer-like day. The meadows were frozen just enough to bear. Examined now the fleets of ice-flakes close at hand. They are a very singular and interesting phenomenon, which I do not remember to have seen. I should say that when the water was frozen about as thick as pasteboard, a violent gust had here and there broken it up, and while the wind and waves held it up on its edge, the increasing cold froze it in firmly. So it seemed, for the flakes were for the most part turned one way; i.e. standing on one side, you saw only their edges, on another-the northeast or southwest-their sides. They were for the most part of a triangular form, like a shoulder[sic]-of-mutton sail, slightly scalloped, like shells. They looked like a fleet of a thousand mackerel-fishers under a press of sail careering before a smacking breeze. Sometimes the sun and wind had reduced them to the thinness of writing-paper, and they fluttered and rustled and tinkled merrily. I skated through them and strewed their wrecks around. They appear to have been elevated expressly to reflect the sun like mirrors, to adorn the river and attract the eye of the skater. Who will say that their principal end is not answered when they excite the admiration of the skater? Every half-mile or mile, as you skate up the river, you see these crystal fleets. Nature is a great imitator and loves to repeat herself.

13 February, 1851, Journal Vol II, 157-158

Rowing up a stream which takes its rise in a mountain, you meet at last with pebbles which have been washed down from it, when many miles distant. I love to think of this kind of introduction to it.

11 June, 1851, Journal Vol II, 244

I pushed out in a boat a little and heard the chopping of the waves under its bow. And on the bottom I saw the moving reflections of the shining wave, faint streaks of light revealing the shadows of the waves or the opaqueness of the water.

13 June, 1851, Journal Vol II, 253

Ah, the very brooks seem fuller of reflections than they were! Ah, such provoking sibylline sentences they are! The shallowest is all at once unfathomable. How can that depth be fathomed where a man may see himself reflected? The rill I stopped to drink at I drink in more than I expected. I satisfy and still provoke the thirst of thirsts. Nut Meadow Brook where it crosses the road beyond Jenny Dugan's that was. I do not drink in vain. I mark that brook as if I had swallowed a water snake that would live in my stomach. I have swallowed something worth the while. The day is not what it was before I stooped to drink. Ah, I shall hear from that draught! It is not in vain that I have drunk. I have drunk an arrowhead. It flows from where all fountains rise.

How many ova have I swallowed? Who knows what will be hatched within me? There were some seeds of thought, methinks, floating in that water, which are expanding in me. The man must not drink of the running streams, the living waters, who is not prepared to have all nature reborn in him, —to suckle monsters. The snake in my stomach lifts his head to my mouth at the sound of running water. When was it that I swallowed a snake? I have got rid of the snake in my stomach. I drank of stagnant waters once. That accounts for it. I caught him by the throat and drew him out, and had a well day after all. Is there not such a thing as getting rid of the snake, which you have swallowed when young, when thoughtless you stooped and drank at stagnant waters, which has worried you in your waking hours and in your sleep ever since, and appropriated the life that was yours? Will he not ascend into your mouth at the sound of running water? Then catch him boldly by the head and draw him out, though you may think his tail be curled about your vitals.

August 17, 1851, Journal Vol II, p417

Our little river reaches are not to be forgotten. I noticed that seen northward on the Assabet from the Causeway Bridge near the second stone bridge. There was [a] man in a boat in the sun, just disappearing in the distance round a bend, lifting high his arms and dipping his paddle as if he were a vision bound to land of the blessed,—far off, as in picture.

23 August, 1851, Journal Vol II, p422-423

As we rowed to fair Haven's eastern shore, a moonlit hill covered with shrub oaks, we could form no opinion of our progress toward it, - not seeing the waterline where it met the hill,—until we saw the weeds and sandy shore and the tall bulrushes rising above the shallow water [like] the masts of large vessels in a haven. The moon was so high that the angle of excidence [sic]did not permit of our seeing her reflection in the pond.

As we paddled down the stream with our backs to the moon, we saw the reflection of every wood and hill on both sides distinctly. These answering reflections—shadow to substance—impress the voyager with a sense of harmony and symmetry, as when you fold a blotted paper and produce a regular figure,—a dualism which nature loves. What you commonly see is but half. Where the shore is very low the actual and reflected trees appear to stand foot to foot, and it is but a line that separates them, and the water and the sky almost flow into one another, and the shore seems to float. As we paddle up or down, we see the cabins of muskrats faintly rising from amid the weeds, and the strong odor of musk is borne to us from particular parts of the shore. Also the odor of a skunk is wafted from over the meadows or fields. The fog appears in some places gathered into a little pyramid or squad by itself, on the surface of the water. Home at ten.

6 October, 1851, Journal Vol III, p51-52

To row a boat thus all the day, with an hour's intermission, making fishes of ourselves as it were, putting on these long fins, realizing the finny life! Surely oars and paddles are but the fins which a man may use.

15 October, 1851, Journal Vol III, p77

When I first paddled a boat on Walden, it was completely surrounded by thick and lofty pine and oak woods, and in some of its coves grape-vines had run over the trees and formed bowers under which a boat could pass. The hills which form its shores are so steep, and the woods on them were then so high, that, as you looked down the pond from west to east, it looked like an ampitheatre [*sic*] for some kind of sylvan spectacle. I have spent many an hour, when I was younger, floating over its surface as the zephyr willed, having paddled to the middle, lying on my back across the seats of my boat, in a summer forenoon, and looking into the sky above, dreaming awake, until I was aroused by my boat touching the sand, and I arose to see what shore my fates had impelled me to; when idleness was the most attractive and productive industry. Many a forenoon have I stolen away thus, preferring thus to spend the most valued part of the day. For I was rich, if not in money, in sunny hours and summer days, and spent them lavishly. Nor do I regret that I did not spend more of them behind a counter or in the workshop or the teacher's desk, in which last two places I have spent so many of them.

25 January, 1852, Journal Vol III, p228-229

Without being the owner of any land, I find I have a civil right in the river, —that, if I am not a landowner I am a water-owner. It is fitting, therefore, that I should have a boat, a cart, for this is my farm. Since it is almost wholly given up to a few of us, while the other highways are much travelled, no wonder that I improve it. Such a one as I will chose to dwell in a township where there are most ponds and rivers and our range is widest. In relation to the river, I find my natural rights least infringed on.

23 March, 1853, Journal Vol V, 45-46

We think it is pleasantest to be on the water at this hour. We row across Fair Haven in the thickening twilight and far below it, steadily and without speaking. As the night draws on the veil, the shores retreat; we only keep in the middle of this low stream of light; we know not whether we float in the air or in the lower region. We seem to recede from the trees on shore or the island very slowly, and yet a few reaches make all our voyage. Nature has divided it agreeably into reaches. The reflections of the stars in the water are dim and elongated like the zodiacal light straight down into the depths, but no mist rises to-night. It is pleasant not to go home till after dark, —to steer by the lights of the vil-lagers. The lamps in the houses twinkle now like stars; they shine doubly bright.

15 October, 1851, Journal Vol III, 78

Last night, as I lay awake, I dreamed of the muddy and weedy river on which I had been paddling, and I seemed to derive some vigor from my day's experience, like the lilies which have their roots at the bottom.

1 July, 1852, Journal Vol IV, 172

It is pleasant to embark on a voyage, if only for a short river excursion, the boat to be your home for the day, especially if it is neat and dry. A sort of moving studio it becomes, you can carry so many things with you. It is almost as if your put oars out at your windows and moved your house along. A sailor, I see, easily becomes attached to his vessel. How continually we [are] thankful to the boat if it does not leak! We move now with a certain pomp and circumstance, with planetary dignity. The pleasure of sailing is akin to that which a planet feels. It seems a more complete adventure than a walk. We make believe embark our all, —our house and furniture. We are further from the earth than the rider; we receive no jar from it. We can carry many things with us.

31 August, 1852, Journal Vol IV, 325

I sat on the Bittern Cliff as the still eve drew on. There was a man on Fair Haven furling his sail and bathing from his boat. A boat on a river whose waters are smoothed, and a man disporting in it! How it harmonizes with the stillness and placidity of the evening! Who knows but he is a poet in his yet obscure but golden youth? Few else go alone into retired scenes without gun or fishing-rod. He bathes in the middle of the pond while his boat slowly drifts away.

2 August, 1854, Journal Vol V, 417

It was in harmony with this fair evening that we were not walking or riding with dust and noise through it, but moved by a paddle without a jar over the liquid and almost invisible surface, floating directly toward those islands of the blessed which we call clouds in the sunset sky. I thought of the Indian, who so many similar evenings had paddled up this stream with what advantage he beheld the twilight sky. So we advanced without dust or sound, by gentle influences, as the twilight gradually faded away. The height of the railroad bridge, already high (more than twenty feet to the top of the rail), was doubled by the reflection, equaling that of a Roman aqueduct, for we could not possibly see where the reflection began, and the piers appeared to rise from the lowest part of the reflection to the rail above, about fifty feet. We floated directly under it, between the piers, as if in mid-air, not being able to distinguish the surface of the water, and looked down more than twenty feet to the reflected flooring through whose intervals we saw the starlit sky. The ghostly piers stretched downward on all sides, and only the angle made by their meeting the real ones betrayed where was the water surface.

7 September, 1854, Journal Vol VII, 20-21

I go across Walden. My shadow is very blue. It is especially blue when there is a bright sunlight on pure white snow. It suggests that there may be something divine, something celestial, in me.

10 February, 1855, Journal Vol VI, 178

Walked as far as Flint's Bridge with Abel Hunt, where I took to the river. I told him I had come to walk on the river as the best place, for the snow had drifted somewhat in the road, while it was converted into ice almost entirely on the river. "But," asked he, "are you not afraid that you will get in?" "Oh, no, it will bear a load of wood from one end to the other." "But then there may be some weak places." Yet he is some seventy years old and was born and bred immediately on its banks. Truly one half the world does not know how the other half lives.

26 January, 1856, Journal Vol VIII, 145

I am encouraged by the sight of the men fishing in Fair Haven Pond, for it reminds me that they have animal spirits for such adventures.

4 January, 1858, Journal Vol X, 235

I think that I speak impartially when I say that I have never met with a stream so suitable for boating and botanizing as the Concord, and fortunately nobody knows it. I know of reaches which a single country-seat would spoil beyond remedy, but there has not been any important change here since I can remember. The willows slumber along its shore, piled in light but low masses, even like the cumuli clouds above. We pass haymakers in every meadow, who may think that we are idlers. But Nature takes care that every nook and crevice is explored by some one. While they look after the open meadows, we farm the tract between the river's brinks and behold the shores from that side.

6 August, 1858, Journal Vol X, 20

It is a fine September day. The river is still rising on account of the rain of the 16th and is getting pretty well over the meadows. As we paddle westward, toward College meadow, I perceive that a new season has come. The air is incredibly clear. The surface of both land and water is bright, as if washed by the recent rain and then seen through a much finer, clearer, and cooler air. The surface of the river sparkles.

18 September, 1858, Journal Vol XI, 162-163

See B. a-fishing notwithstanding the wind. A man runs down, fails, loses self-respect, and goes a-fishing, though he were never seen on the river before. Yet methinks his "misfortune" is good for him, and he is the more mellow and humane. Perhaps he begins to perceive more clearly that the object of life is something else than acquiring property, and he really stands in a truer relation to his fellow-men than when he commanded a false respect of them. There he stands at length, perchance better employed than ever, holding communion with nature and himself and coming to understand his real position and relation to men in this world. It is better than a poor debtors' prison, better than most successful money-getting.

4 October, 1858, Journal Vol XI, 196

A new phase of the spring is presented; a new season has come. By the soaking rain and the wind of yesterday especially, the remaining snow and ice has been almost entirely swept away, and the ice has been broken, floated off, and melted, and much frost taken out of the ground; and now, as we glide over the Great Meadows before this strong wind, we no longer see dripping saturated russet and brown banks through rain, hearing at intervals the alarm notes of the early robins, —banks which reflect a yellowish light, —but we see the bare and now pale-brown and dry russet hills. The earth has cast off her white coat and come forth in her clean-washed sober russet early spring dress. As we look over the lively, tossing blue waves for a mile or more eastward and northward, our eyes fall on these shining russet hills, and Ball's Hill appears in this strong light at the verge of this undulating blue plain, like some glorious newly created island of the spring, just sprung up from the bottom in the midst of the blue waters. The fawn-colored oak leaves, with a few pines intermixed, thickly covering the hill, look not like a withered vegetation, but an ethereal kind, just expanded and peculiarly adapted to the season and the sky.

Look toward the sun, the water is yellow, as water in which the earth has just washed itself clean of its winter impurities; look from the sun and it is a beautiful dark blue; but in each direction the crests of the waves are white, and you cannot sail or row over this watery wilderness without sharing the excitement of this element. Our sail draws so strongly that we cut through the great waves without feeling them.

16 March, 1859, Journal Vol XII, 49-50

To-day we sail swiftly on dark rolling waves or paddle over a sea as smooth as a mirror, unable to touch the bottom, where mowers work and hide their jugs in August; coasting the edge of maple swamps, where alder tassels and white maple flowers are kissing the tide that has risen to meet them. But this particular phase of beauty is fleeting. Nature has so many shows for us she cannot afford to give much time to this. In a few days, perchance, these lakes will have all run away to the sea. Such are the pictures which she paints. When we look at our masterpieces we see only dead paint and its vehicle, which suggests no liquid life rapidly flowing off from beneath.

28 March, 1859, Journal Vol XII, 95-96

The fisherman stands erect and still on the ice, awaiting our approach, as usual forward to say that he has had no luck. He has been here since early morning, won't catch him here again in a hurry. They all tell the same story. The amount of it is he has had "fisherman's luck," and if you walk that way you may find him at his old post to-morrow. It is hard, to be sure, —four little fishes to be divided between three men, and two and a half miles to walk; and you have only got a more ravenous appetite for the supper which you have not earned. However, the pond floor is not a bad place to spend a winter day.

22 December, 1859, Journal Vol XIII, 39

I walk over a smooth green sea, or aequor, the sun just disappearing in the cloudless horizon, amid thousands of these flat isles as purple as the petals of a flower. It would not be more enchanting to walk amid the purple clouds of the sunset sky. And, by the way, this is but a sunset sky under our feet, produced by the same law, the same slanting rays and twilight. Here the clouds are these patches of snow or frozen vapor, and the ice is the greenish sky between them. Thus all of heaven is realized on earth. You have seen those purple fortunate isles in the sunset heavens, and that green and amber sky between them. Would you believe that you could ever walk amid those isles? You can on many a winter evening. I have done so a hundred times. The ice is a solid crystalline sky under our feet.

12 February, 1860, Journal Vol XIII, 140-141

Not only the earth but the heavens are made our footstool. That is what the phenomenon of ice means. The earth is annually inverted and we walk upon the sky. The ice reflects the blue of sky. The waters become solid and make a sky below. The clouds grow heavy and fall to earth, and we walk on them. We live and walk on solidified fluids.

12 February, 1860, Journal Vol XIII, 141

Sometimes, after staying in the village parlor till the family had all retired, I have returned to the woods, and, partly with a view to the next day's dinner, spent the hours of midnight fishing from a boat by moonlight, serenaded by owls and foxes, and hearing, from time to time, the creaking note of some unknown bird close at hand. These experiences were very memorable and valuable to me, —anchored in forty feet of water, and twenty of thirty rods from the shore, surrounded sometimes by thousands of small perch and shiners, dimpling the surface with their tails in the moonlight, and communicating by a long flaxen line with mysterious nocturnal fishes which had their dwelling forty feet below, or sometimes dragging sixty feet of line about the pond as I drifted in the gentle night breeze, now and then feeling a slight vibration along it, indicative of some life prowling about its extremity, of dull uncertain blundering purpose there, and slow to make up its mind. At length you slowly raise, pulling hand over hand, some horned pout squeaking and squirming to the upper air. It was very queer, especially in dark nights, when your thoughts had wandered to vast and cosmogonal themes in other spheres, to feel this faint jerk, which came to interrupt your dreams and link you to Nature again. It seemed as if I might next cast my line upward into the air, as well as downward into this element which was scarcely more dense. Thus I caught two fishes as it were with one hook.

Walden, 113-114

One November afternoon, in the calm at the end of a rain storm of several days' duration, when the sky was still completely overcast and the air was full of mist, I observed that the pond was remarkably smooth, so that it was difficult to distinguish its surface; though it no longer reflected the bright tints of October, but the sombre November color of the surrounding hills. Though I passed over it as gently as possible, the slight undulations produced by my boat extended almost as far as I could see, and gave a ribbed appearance to the reflections. But, as I was looking over the surface, I saw here and there at a distance a faint glimmer, as if some skater insects which had escaped the frosts might be collected there, or, perchance, the surface, being so smooth, betrayed where a spring welled up from the bottom. Paddling gently to one of these places, I was surprised to find myself surrounded by myriads of small perch, about five inches long, of a rich bronze color in the green water, sporting there and constantly rising to the surface and dimpling it, sometimes leaving bubbles on it. In such transparent and seemingly bottomless water, reflecting the clouds, I seemed to be floating through the air as in a balloon, and their swimming impressed me as a kind of flight or hovering, as if they were a compact flock of birds passing just beneath my level on the right or left, their fins, like sails, set all around them.

Walden, 123

I have spent many an hour, when I was younger, floating over its surface as the zephyr willed, having paddled my boat to the middle, and lying on my back across the seats, in a summer forenoon, dreaming awake, until I was aroused by the boat touching the sand, and I arose to see what shore my fates had impelled me to; days when idleness was the most attractive and productive industry. Many a forenoon have I stolen away, pre-ferring to spend thus the most valued part of the day; for I was rich, if not in money, in sunny hours and summer days, and spent them lavishly; nor do I regret that I did not waste more of them in the workshop or the teacher's desk.

Walden, 125

Then to my morning work. First I take an axe and pail and go in search of water, if that be not a dream. After a cold and snowy night it needed a divining rod to find it. Every winter the liquid and trembling surface of the pond, which was so sensitive to every breath, and reflected every light and shadow, becomes solid to the depth of a foot or a foot and a half, so that it will support the heaviest teams, and perchance the snow covers it to an equal depth, and it is not to be distinguished from any level field. Like the marmots in the surrounding hills, it closes its eyelids and becomes dormant for three months or more. Standing on the snow-covered plain, as if in a pasture amid the hills, I cut my way first though a foot of snow, and then a foot of ice, and open a window under my feet, where, kneeling to drink, I look down in onto the quiet parlor of the fishes, pervaded by a softened light as through a window of ground glass, with its bright sanded floor the same as in summer; there a perennial waveless serenity reigns as in the amber twilight sky, corresponding to the cool and even temperament of the inhabitants. Heaven is under our feet as well as over our heads.

Walden, 182

Gradually the village murmur subsided, and we seemed to be embarked on the placid current of our dreams, floating from past to future as silently as one awakes to fresh morning or evening thoughts. We glided noiselessly down the stream, occasionally driving a pickerel from the covert of the pads, or a bream from her nest, and the smaller bittern now and then sailed away on sluggish wings from some recess in the shore, or the larger lifted itself out of the long grass at our approach, and carried its precious legs away to deposit them in a place of safety.

A Week, 17

The last vestiges of daylight at length disappeared, and as we rowed silently along with our backs toward home through the darkness, only a few stars being visible, we had little to say, but sat absorbed in thought, or in silence listened to the monotonous sound of our oars, a sort of rudimental music, suitable for the ear of Night and the acoustics of her dimly lighted halls.

A Week, 488

The river flows in the rear of the towns, and we see all things from a new and wilder side. The fields and gardens come down to it with a frankness, and freedom from pretension, which they do not wear on the highway. It is the outside and edge of the earth. Our eyes are not offended by violent contrasts. The last rail of the farmer's fence is some swaying willow bough, which still preserves its freshness, and here at length all fences stop, and we no longer cross any road. We may go far up within the country now by the most retired and level road, never climbing a hill, but by broad levels ascending to the upland meadows. It is a beautiful illustration of the law of obedience, the flow of a river; the path for a sick man, a highway down which an acorn cup may float secure with its freight. Its slight occasional falls, whose precipices would not diversify the landscape, are celebrated by mist and spray, and attract the traveler from far and near. From the remote interior, its current conducts him by broad and easy steps, or by one gentler inclined plane, to the sea. Thus by an early and constant yielding to the inequalities of the ground it secures itself the easiest passage.

A Winter Walk, 65-66

When I got to the river the day after the principal fall of leaves, the sixteenth, I find my boat all covered, bottom and seats, with the leaves of the golden willow under which it is moored, and I set sail with a cargo of them rustling under my feet. If I empty it, it will be full again to-morrow. I do not regard them as litter, to be swept out, but accept them as suitable straw or matting for the bottom of my carriage. When I turn up into the mouth of the Assabet, which is wooded, large fleets of leaves are floating on its surface, as it were getting out to sea, with room to tack; but next the shore, a little farther up, they are thicker than foam, quite concealing the water for a rod in width, under and amid the alders, button-bushes, and maples, still perfectly light and dry, with fibre unrelaxed; and at a rocky bend where they are met and stopped by the morning wind, they sometimes form a broad and dense crescent quite across the river. When I turn my prow that way, and the wave which it makes strikes them, list what a pleasant rustling from these dry substances getting on one another! Often it is their undulation only which reveals the water beneath them. Also every motion of the wood turtle on the shore is betrayed by their rustling there. Or even in mid-channel, when the wind rises, I hear them blown with a rustling sound. Higher up they are slowly moving round and round in some great eddy which the river makes, as that at the "Leaning Hemlocks," where the water is deep, and the current is wearing into the bank.

Perchance, in the afternoon of such a day, when the water is perfectly calm and full of reflections, I paddle gently down the main stream, and turning up the Assabet, reach a quiet cove, where I unexpectedly find myself surrounded by myriads of leaves, like fellow-voyagers, which seem to have the same purpose, or want of purpose, with myself. See this great fleet of scattered leaf-boats which we paddle amid, in this smooth river-bay, each one curled up on every side by the sun's skill, each nerve a stiff spruce knee, —like boats of hide, and of all patterns, —Charon's boat probably among the rest, —and some with lofty prows and poops, like the stately vessels of the ancients, scarcely moving in the sluggish current, —like the great fleets, the dense Chinese cities of boats, with which you mingle on entering some great mart, some New York or Canton, which we are all steadily approaching together. How gently each has been deposited on the water! No violence has been used towards them yet, though, perchance, palpitating hearts were present at the launching. And painted ducks, to, the splendid wood duck among the rest, often come to sail and float amid the painted leaves, —barks of a nobler model still!

Autumnal Tints, 154-156

It is wonderful how well watered this country is. As you paddle across a lake, bays will be pointed out to you, by following up which, and perhaps the tributary stream which empties in, you may, after a short portage, or possibly, at some seasons, none at all, get into another river, which empties far away from the one you are on. Generally, you may go in any direction in a canoe, by making frequent but not very long portages. You are only realizing once more what all nature distinctly remembers here, for no doubt the waters flowed thus in a former geological period, and instead of being a lake country, it was an archipelago. It seems as if the more youthful and impressible streams can hardly resist the numerous invitations and temptations to leave their native beds and run down their neighbors' channels.

The Maine Woods, 245-246

After this rough walking in the dark woods it was an agreeable change to glide down the rapid river in the canoe once more. This river, which was about the size of our Assabet (in Concord), though still very swift, was almost perfectly smooth here, and showed a very visible declivity, a regularly inclined plane, for several miles, like a mirror set a little aslant, on which we coasted down. This very obvious regular descent, particularly plain when I regarded the water-line against the shores, made a singular impression on me, which the swiftness of our motion probably enhanced, so that we seemed to be gliding down a much steeper declivity than we were, and that we could not save ourselves from rapids and falls if we should suddenly come to them. My companion did not perceive this slope, but I have a surveyor's eyes, and I satisfied myself that it was not ocular illusion. You could tell at a glance on approaching such a river, which way the water flowed, though you might perceive no motion. I observed the angle at which a level line would strike the surface, and calculated the amount of fall in a rod, which did not need to be remarkably great to produce this effect.

It was very exhilarating, and the perfection of travelling, quite unlike floating on our dead Concord River, the coasting down this inclined mirror, which was now and then gently winding, down a mountain, indeed, between two evergreen forests,

111

edged with lofty dead white pines, sometimes slanted half-way over the stream, and destined soon to bridge it.

The Maine Woods, 251-252

The genius of Thoreau is that, although he clearly reveled in his watery exploits for their very own merits, he was also able to call upon this close and personal immersion as the vehicle from which to inspire his environmental pursuits of preserving free and untainted water. The interlinking of personal explorations of riverways with an understanding of how that may be used to develop a codex of natural "rights" is a subject that has often been articulated by the eminent wilderness scholar Roderick Nash.
–RLF

Afterword

The extraordinary intellectual revolution that, over the last several centuries, transformed wilderness from a liability into an asset was largely anthropocentric. Wild land was valued and preserved for people. Recreational, spiritual and scenic values all used man as the measure. So did the early ecological arguments with their utilitarian emphasis on protecting species that possibly held "the cure for cancer." More recently, wild ecosystems have been praised as "resources" capable of providing environmental "services" to people. These are the arguments that sell nature protection on the political stage.

What is remarkable about Henry David Thoreau is that his defense of wild nature moved beyond anthropocentrism—from a utilitarian to an intrinsic valuation. He understood that wilderness was not "for" people at all. It was, he explained, the home of civilization other than our own. Their rights were important. Society and morality, in his mind, were not concerned exclusively with those kinds of beings called human.

The present book concerns Thoreau's relationship to water. The management and control (read "dams, ditches and drains") of water has been a centerpiece of the human crusade to conquer and dominate nature. Robert France knows well that Thoreau was a proto-ecologist whose thinking did not draw lines through the natural community. It followed that rivers, for example, were not "dead" but living processes, inextricably connected to the web of life. As such they deserved moral respect and legal protection.

Thoreau's ethical opposition to slavery is well known. But he also opposed the enslavement of nature and, in particular, rivers. In 1849 he lamented a new dam on the Concord River that prevented the "poor shad" from completing their ancestral spawning run. "Who hears the fishes when they cry?" he lamented. This train of thought led Thoreau to what a later generation would call "environmental radicalism" (or in Edward Abbey's 1960s term, "monkey-wrenching") and he speculated on the effects of a crowbar on the Bellerica Dam. Although they thought in terms of explosives, dam opponents of the next century followed Thoreau in his moral outrage of the treatment of nature and his willingness to transcend the law in its liberation. In 1981, Dave Foreman called on fellow eco-warriors to "free shackled rivers." Abbey explained that ethics should extend "to the non-living, the inorganic, to the springs, streams, lakes, rivers and oceans."

No doubt Thoreau somewhere nods in agreement. He led the American recognition that natural rights should evolve to include the rights of nature.

—Roderick Frazier Nash

References

Works by Thoreau

A Week on the Concord and Merrimack Rivers. C. Leighton, ed. Parnassus Imprints, 1987.

Cape Cod. J. J. Moldenhauer, ed. Princeton University Press. 1988.

The Correspondence of Henry David Thoreau. W. Harding and C. Bode, eds. New York University Press, 1958.

The Journal of Henry David Thoreau. Volumes I - XIV. B. Torrey and F.H. Allen, eds. Houghton Mifflin, 1906.

The Maine Woods. J. J. Moldenhauser, ed. Princeton University Press, 1972.

The Natural History Essays. R. Sattelmeyer, ed. Peregrine Smith, 1980.

The Writings of Henry David Thoreau. V. Excursions and Poems. AMS Press, 1968.

Walden. L.D. Stanley, ed. Princeton University Press, 1971.

Works About Thoreau

The following sources were instrumental in formulating the ideas contained within the Introduction, and to these scholars I am extremely grateful.

Bonner, Willard H. *Harp on the Shore: Thoreau and the Sea.* State University of New York Press, 1985.

Channing, William E. *Thoreau: The Poet-Naturalist.* Roberts Brothers, 1873.

Dean, Bradley P., ed. *Faith in a Seed: The Dispersion of Seeds and Other Late Natural History Writings*. Island Press, 1993.

Dean, Bradley P. "A walk to Thoreau's bean field." 60th Annual Gathering of The Thoreau Society, Concord, MA, July 2001.

Friesen, Victor C. *The Spirit of the Huckleberry: Sensuousness in Henry Thoreau*. The University of Alberta Press, 1984.

France, Robert L. *Reflecting Heaven: Thoreau on Water*. Houghton Mifflin, 2001.

France, Robert L. *Water-logged-in: A Dynamic Library of Aquatic Quotations from Thoreau's Descendents*. An e-book at www.water-logged-in.com. 2001.

Garber, Frederick. *Thoreau's Redemptive Imagination*. New York University Press, 1977.

Harding, Walter. *The Days of Henry Thoreau: A Biography*. Dover Publications, 1982.

Hildebidle, John. *Thoreau: A Naturalist's Liberty*. Harvard University Press, 1983.

Huber, J. Parker. *The Wildest Country: A Guide to Thoreau's Maine*. Appalachian Club, 1981.

Jorgenson, N. *A Guide to New England's Landscape*. Barre Publ., 1971.

Lunt, Dudley C., ed. *Henry David Thoreau: The River*. Wayne Publ. 1963.

McGregor, Robert K. *A Wider View of the Universe: Henry Thoreau's Study of Nature*. University of Illinois Press, 1997.

McIntosh, James. *Thoreau as Romantic Naturalist: His Shifting Stance Toward Nature*. Cornell University Press, 1974.

Milder, Robert. *Reimagining Thoreau*. Cambridge University Press, 1995.

Paul, Sherman. *The Shores of America: Thoreau's Inward Exploration*. University of Illinois Press, 1958.

Richardson, Robert D., Jr. *Henry Thoreau: A Life of the Mind*. University of California Press, 1998.

Schneider, Richard J., ed. *Thoreau's Sense of Place: Essays in American Environmental Writing*. University of Iowa Press, 2000.

Walls, Laura D. *Seeing New Worlds: Henry David Thoreau and Nineteenth-Century Natural Science.* The University of Wisconsin Press, 1995.

Walls, Laura D. "Thoreau, poetry and science." 60th Annual Gathering The Thoreau Society. Concord, MA, July 2001.

Worster, Donald. *Nature's Economy: A History of Ecological Ideas.* Cambridge University Press, 1977.

Acknowledgments

Kjersti Monson and Leslie Zucker aided in manuscript preparation. This project was funded in part by operating grants from the Harvard Design School. I would like to thank Parker Huber, David Kidner, John Middendorf, John Mitchell, Laura Sewall, and especially Ann Zwinger and Roderick Nash—impassioned lovers of, and enthusiastic dabblers in, waters all—for their thoughtful and inspiring words.

For more on water in literature, browse *Water-logged-in.com: A Dynamic Library of Aquatic Quotations from Thoreau's Descendants*, an eBook published at:

water-logged-in.com

"These quotations are a potent reminder to get outside, to get dirty, to get wet, and to rejoice in your lived experience. They should catalyze action, spur you to taste the world, and remember that you are part of nature. And when you return form your adventure, you will be changed for the better…Read these quotations. Enjoy these stories of those who came before you. You will be enobled."

—*Robert Abbott, Abbott Strategies*

"While Water-logged-in claims to offer non-fiction quotations as literary solace in an age of information saturation, its true passion flows directly from France's faith in the restorative power of aquatic immersion…In aggregate, the quotations in Water-logged-in bear compelling witness to the centrality of water in any understanding of human nature…Water-logged-in prompts no less than immersion itself, be it of the intellectual or the embodied sort. As the quotations at the heart of this collection suggest, however, the best sort of dips will be both."

—*Cheryl Foster, University of Rhode Island*

"Robert France has brought luminous water voices together into the most dynamic library imaginable. Enjoy the adventure, the joy, the contact and contemplation, and the mystery of water."

—*Grant Jones, Jones & Jones Architects and Landscape Architects*

Water-logged-in.com was prepared as a reader for a course at Harvard Universtiy, *Ecopsychology: Human–Nature Relationships.*

GREEN FRIGATE BOOKS

"THERE IS NO FRIGATE LIKE A BOOK"

Words on the page have the power to transport us, and in the process, transform us. Such journeys can be far reaching, traversing the landscapes of the external world and that within, as well as the timescapes of the past, present and future.

Green Frigate Books is a small publishing house offering a vehicle—a ship—for those seeking to conceptually sail and explore the horizons of the natural and built environments, and the relations of humans within them. Our goal is to reach an educated lay readership by producing works that fall in the cracks between those offered by traditional academic and popular presses.